This Means WAR!

The Seed Of The Righteous Shall Be Delivered

A Biblical Perspective On Adult Child Parent Estrangement

Angeline L. Williams

Copyright © 2022 Angeline L. Williams

All rights reserved.

ISBN: 978-1-7325258-4-9

All rights reserved. No part of this publication may be reproduced, stored in a retrieval system, or transmitted in any form or by any means electronic, mechanical, digital, photocopy, recording, or any other except for brief quotation in printed reviews, without the written permission of the publisher.

DISCLAIMER: THIS BOOK DOES NOT PROVIDE MEDICAL ADVICE. However, the author does attempt to answer questions and suggest things you can do to change and heal (mind, soul and body) based on the Word of God.

Dedication

This book is dedicated to every parent who is experiencing the heart-wrenching pain of being estranged from their adult children and grandchildren.

Table of Contents

Dedication 3

Table of Contents 4

Introduction 7

Blood Isn't Always Thicker Than Water 12

About Adult Child Parent Estrangement 23

   The Root of Adult Child Parent Estrangement 25

Walking In Truth 30

   Making Amends 32

   Forgiveness Is Necessary 38

   Rejection From The Womb 46

Guilt, Shame, and Condemnation 59

   Guilt 59

   Shame 60

   Condemnation 61

   Reaping What You Sow 61

- Stay Alert 68
- Breaking Generational Cycles 72
  - Pull Down Strongholds That Pull You Down 76
  - Our Powerful Armor 79
- God's Sovereign Will 88
  - Trust The Process 92
  - Beauty for Ashes 97
  - Let Go and Let God 101
- Remove The Grave Clothes 111
  - Praying With Holy Anger 114
- Valley Of Dry Bones 121
  - Pray The Word of God Over Your Adult Children 127
- Sometimes You Will Have To Encourage Yourself 132
- Scriptures and Prayers 137
  - Scriptures To Pray Over Your Children 139
  - Scriptures to Declare for Family Healing 144
  - Psalm 91 Prayer Confession 149
  - Prayer To Restore Broken Family Relationships 151

    Struggling With Unforgiveness Prayer 153

    Prayer For Healing From Rejection 155

    Prayer to Forgive Someone 157

Prodigals Coming Home 160

Final Thoughts 163

About The Author 167

Introduction

When my kids were young, I looked forward to Sunday dinners and family gatherings with my children and grandchildren. Not once did I imagine having a daughter pass on to eternal life, and having my remaining children not speaking to me, and having no interaction with most of my grandchildren.

Some of the most painful things a parent can go through is watching a child go down a path of destruction, the death of a child, and their adult child estranging them. These things can weigh heavily on the heart of a parent like nothing else. With each birthday and holiday missed, hateful word spoken, and unyielding silence, the knife is twisted deeper into the wound.

It is natural to grieve the loss, but you don't want it to control your life. Grief can cause you to struggle with anger, fear, or depression. Some find themselves seeking relief in destructive activities, such as abusing alcohol, drugs, or food, and avoiding daily responsibilities. These activities never help. They only add to the problems.

I have talked with several mothers whose adult children have estranged them. Both my sons have estranged me, and my only daughter has gone home to be with the Lord. So, I understand the deep pain that a mother experiences when her child, that she raised, and loves, wants nothing to do with her. This is a pain I want no parent to experience. Sadly, in this day, many mothers and fathers do.

After talking with many parents, mainly mothers whose children have alienated them and experiencing it myself, I realized that estrangement is prevalent in the world today. One psychiatrist even calls it a "silent epidemic." Another said that adult children being estranged from their parents is perhaps as common as divorce in certain segments of society. All of this was very disheartening and somewhat encouraging at the same time. It let me know that I am not the only mother enduring hatred from her own children.

I sought God about why this evil is so prevalent

today. How do we stand in faith in the midst of it? How do we pray for our family, and our adult children, to be delivered from this evil? The more I prayed and studied, the more God revealed to me. Estrangement happens between siblings and other family members. However, I am only addressing adult child and parent estrangement.

In Hosea 4:6, God said we are *"destroyed for lack of knowledge."* So many Believers in Christ lose battles they should win because they don't know the Word of God, and are not aware of the power of God in them. If you don't know and believe the Word of God, who you are in Christ, and what Christ has made available for you, then you cannot possess what belongs to you. You will lose the battles of sickness, addiction, financial lack, family destruction, and every other battle that the devil brings to you. If you want your family restored, your best defense is knowing and believing the Word of God, and how to wield your Sword, and understanding how your personal adversary operates.

One promise that I firmly stand on is in the title of this book, which is found in Proverbs 11:21, "The seed of the righteous shall be delivered." Righteous means justified and vindicated by God. Those of us in Christ are righteous because of what Jesus did on the cross. The word "deliver" means "to escape and rescue." Seed is our offspring. I take God at His word, so I am confident that my seed shall be delivered, that they will come to themselves and escape whatever bondage, trap and snare Satan has set up for them.

This book is for parents whose children have estranged them. In this book, I share what God shared with me regarding adult child parent estrangement to strengthen and help parents walk through this difficult valley and fight for their family and the souls of their children. All parents should be prayer warriors, interceding for their children and their bloodline.

Satan has come against the structure of the Divine Family of God, but Satan shall not continue to destroy our family, neither shall he have our children. This means war, and God has given His children the tools to win the battle. Together we are going to learn why this estrangement is happening, and how to stand and intercede and praise God for our children's deliverance from Satan's deception!!

Although God rains on the just and the unjust, the benefits and blessings of the Cross belong to the Believers of Christ. I invite anyone who has never accepted Jesus Christ as Savior and Lord to do that now. Because the most important thing in life is where you spend eternity, the most important decision you will ever make is accepting Jesus as Lord.

Without Jesus, we will spend eternity in hell, but with Him, we will spend eternity in heaven. If you've never accepted Jesus as your Savior and Lord, and you believe that Jesus went to the Cross, died, and rose on the third day, then pray this prayer with me out loud.

Heavenly Father, I invite Jesus Christ into my life as my Savior. I believe Jesus died for my sins and rose from the dead. The blood of Jesus cleanses me from all my sins, and from this moment forward, I'm a child of God.

If you prayed that prayer and meant it, you just made the greatest decision of your life. I praise God for you and welcome to the family of God.

Blood Isn't Always Thicker Than Water

For years, my sons and I have not been close, but at least we did have some contact with one another. Both of them left home at an early age and went into the military. They were overseas most of the time, or stationed away from home, so I reasoned that this was why we weren't close. I would say we just don't know each other.

I was a single parent raising three children with no assistance from their fathers. My house was the house where my kids and their friends hung out. I was the mom who drove them and their friends where they wanted to hang out. I tried to be there for them as much as possible. I did things with each of them separately one Saturday a month to spend quality time with each of them.

I am not trying to exaggerate, or make it seem as if things were peachy cream, because they weren't. I struggled financially, and we moved a lot.

I tried to keep them in decent neighborhoods because I did not want them to become involved in gangs and drugs. I tried to get them most of the material things they wanted and needed, and I brought them up in church and taught them about Christ.

In my mind, I was a pretty good mother. Not a perfect mother, but not a horrible mother, either. For me, the good outweighs the bad. For them, it seems the bad outweighs the good. Nothing occurred that I am aware of that warrants the estrangement. I've asked over and over if something happened to them as children that I missed, if they were molested. The answer was always no.

Because we moved so much during those years of struggle, I dealt with a lot of shame and ridicule. Rumors spread about me, and a lot of ugly things were said about me by people in my church. I couldn't afford to be out of work, so I worked a lot of temporary jobs. When the job ended, I moved on to another. Instead of asking me what happened, people said I couldn't hold on to a job. I was accused of being an unfit mother, and one of the leaders of the church even voiced this to my son.

My children experienced shame and ridicule

too, but they never discussed it with me. One day, just before he cut me out of his life, in a fit of rage, my youngest son said that he had always been ashamed of me. When he said that, it crushed me. He told me that I am dead to him, and he is mourning my funeral now, because he will not be there when I die. He doesn't want me to have anything to do with him or his family.

A few months later, my oldest son sent me a text saying, "I'm going to need you to no longer pray for me. Respect my wishes. I don't find any power in the way you pray. In fact, I feel that it is more harm than helpful. Thank you. I have tried to love you, but I realize I don't love you. You are poisonous to my soul. I can't hold on to you anymore. So now you have lost me, too."

When my oldest on sent the text that seemed to come out of nowhere, I was shocked. My mind was whirling, trying to figure out how they could feel this way, and say those things to me. Me, the one who sacrificed so that they could have. Me, the one who believed that despite the struggle, I was blessed to have my children. Me, the one who was proud of them and bragged about their accomplishments. Me, the one who invested my life into them, only to have them become adults and turn away from me and each other.

As you can imagine, the words both my sons said to me hurt deeply, but I realized that my sons were hurting. It's ironic, that we are most hurtful to others when we are in pain ourselves. You have heard the saying, "hurt people, hurt people," right? It is just as strange that we usually lash out at those we love the most. We may not see it because of the rejection we are receiving from our children, but the pain cuts both ways.

It was not my choice to sever the relationship with my sons, and it is probably not your choice that you and your child are estranged either. I want you to understand that, even though you made mistakes, you are not responsible for your child's choice. I also want you to understand that severing ties with their parents is not easy for adult children.

Before your child made the decision, they may have agonized over it for quite a while. Keep in mind that the same devil that came and interfered with your family wants to destroy every member of your family. Your child may put on a front and act as if the situation doesn't bother them, but it does. They are hurting too. They just don't know how to come back.

Even with this knowledge, and as much as I tried not to allow it, the troubled relationship between my sons and me was beginning to consume me. I started experiencing the same grief I experienced when my daughter passed on to eternal life, but I don't blame my children. It was not my sons saying such hurtful and foolish things to me. My sons do not speak to me and disrespect me in that way, but Satan, the accuser of the brethren, does.

The Bible clearly speaks about the reality of spiritual warfare. The Word of God would not mention spiritual warfare if it were not a reality. We can ignore it, and pretend spiritual warfare doesn't exist, but it doesn't change the fact that it does. Paul, in Ephesians 6:12 warns, *"For we wrestle not against flesh and blood, but against principalities, against powers, against the rulers of the darkness of this world, against spiritual wickedness in high places."*

In this passage, Paul is talking about spiritual warfare. Understand that your child is not your enemy. Neither is your child's spouse, nor any other human being. No! The devil and his demons are your enemies. And they will use everyone and everything they can to distract, discourage, and destroy you. Especially the people you love most. He wants us to view our family members as our enemies, because if we are busy fighting each other, then we will not form a united front against him.

People have been so programmed to believe that other people are responsible for their problems that they find it difficult to believe this truth. Some people have even been deceived into believing that God is the cause of their problems. God is not your enemy, either! If you are born again, God is your Father, and His thoughts for you are thoughts of good, never of evil (Jeremiah 29:11). There is no darkness in God, and there is no light in the devil. I want you to understand how much the devil hates you, and I want you to understand that we are doing battle with spiritual entities. Just as God is light, Satan, the devil, is darkness.

Estrangement is tough. In the midst of your pain, it may be difficult to get past the hurt your child has caused. For me, understanding who is instigating it helps me. I believe if you recognize who is really behind the words and actions of your child, it will help you too. Satan hates everything God created. He hates marriage, the family, and the seed of the woman, especially since God made the promise that the seed of woman would destroy him.

Declare... God brought my child here for a purpose, and the will of God in their life shall be done here on earth as it is in heaven.

I am not saying that my sons, or your child, is possessed by the devil or anything like that. What I am saying is, Satan will use whoever yields themselves to him (Romans 6:16), saved or unsaved, knowingly or unknowingly. He is the father of lies. He perverts what really happened, and continuously pumps his lies into the head of any person who will listen to him. Then he preys on the pain he has caused to get them to carry out his character, and bring about division, and ultimately destruction. If only people could see how they are being played like puppets on a string, this destruction could end.

If a lie is told long enough, after a while, the majority of people will begin to believe it, unless they have the discernment of the Holy Spirit. The more the lie spreads, the more the lie appears to be the truth. I know it's easier said than done, but don't take your child's rejection personally. Don't make it about you, make it only about the deception they have prey fallen to. That way, you won't become angry with them, and you will show mercy towards them and pray for them.

When you feel yourself getting sad, and when they cross your mind, pray, and then praise God for the answer. Decree God's Word over the situation. When my son texted and requested that I stop praying for him, it confirmed to me that my prayer and standing in faith is working. The effective, fervent prayer of a righteous man avails much (James 5:16).

As Believers, we are covered under the blood of Jesus, and we have authority through Christ Jesus. Next to introducing our children to Christ, I believe the next best thing a parent can do for their child is to intercede for them, even if their child is grown. The fervent prayer of a parent is powerful. Don't ever allow the enemy to make you so angry with your child, that you will not pray for them. Don't let anyone tell you that God doesn't want you to pray for your child. Don't let Satan or anyone tell you that the relationship with your child is a hopeless case. He is a liar! Shout to the gates of hell, *"The seed of the righteous shall be delivered!" Halleluiah!*

Why am I so candid about my life? It is not to inflict pain or bring embarrassment on myself or my sons. Long ago, God told me when I preach and write to be transparent. People need to know that He is a tangible God who loves and cares about every area of our lives. We are never alone. He is with us through everything we go through, and He will take the good and the bad and work them together for our good.

Also, I want you to understand what and who we are dealing with and where estrangement comes from. It is not your children, no matter what they do or say. It is Satan who has come to steal, kill, and destroy your family. I will not allow the devil to make me feel ashamed of what he is doing. I will not crawl into a corner, cower, or hide. I will expose him, and how he's trying to tear down families and steal our children, and take them to hell with him. He is a liar! In the midst of waiting on God to deliver my sons, I will help others stand up and fight for their family too!

So, if you are feeling ashamed of what is happening between you and your adult children, let me let you in on a secret. There are no perfect families, and there are no perfect Christians. All families have disagreements and days when one member might not speak to another. I have talked to many Believers who have family problems, just like you and me.

So, if Satan is telling you that no one will understand, and that you aren't a good Christian because you and your children don't get along, he is a liar, and he is at the root of the problem. God loves you, and He wants to set you and your family free. With God, all things are possible for those who believe. There is hope. Your family situation is not hopeless. You and your family can move on from estrangement to unity and love.

Believers are never powerless against what the enemy does in our life. If you stand on God's Word, you will win. Satan's days are numbered. His fate has been set. There is no restoration for him! Jesus Christ has won the victory. He has defeated Satan and disarmed the spiritual rulers and authorities. He shamed them publicly by His (Jesus') victory over them on the cross. (Colossians 2:15) Satan will be thrown into the lake of fire! Satan's days are numbered and so is his attack against you and your children.

> *"[10] The devil, who deceived them, was cast into the lake of fire and brimstone where the beast and the false prophet are. And they will be tormented day and night forever and ever. [11] Then I saw a great white throne and Him who sat on it, from whose face the earth and the heaven fled away. And there was found no place for them. [12] And I saw the dead, small and great, standing before God, and books were opened. And another book was opened, which is the Book of Life. And the dead were judged according to their works, by the things which were written in the books. [13] The sea gave up the dead who were in it, and Death and Hades delivered up the dead who were in them. And they were judged, each one according to his works. [14] Then Death and Hades were cast into the lake of fire. This is the second death."* – Revelation 20:10-14 NKJV

About Adult Child Parent Estrangement

"And above all these put on love, which binds everything together in perfect harmony." – *Colossians 3:14*

What is adult child parent estrangement? The dictionary defines estranged as having lost former closeness and affection, or being alienated from a close or familial relationship. Adult child parent estrangement is when an adult child alienates themselves from their parents. When your child cuts you out of their life, it causes a lot of pain, heartache, shame, guilt, grief, confusion, and more.

Because people have such strong opinions and emotions about adult child parent estrangement, it has a horrible stigma attached to it. Most parents I've talked with are reluctant to talk about what's happening with them and their children, and with good reason. Most people judge you, and presume that you must be a terrible parent for your child to cut you off like that. They believe what the adult child says whether it is true or not.

Adult child parent estrangement doesn't just happen to bad parents. Most parents of estranged adult children are loving, well-meaning parents who have made many sacrifices for their children, and tried their best to provide a good home for them. Sadly, something went terribly wrong. Many times, the estranged parent is left trying to figure out what went wrong, and blaming themselves, believing they failed as a parent.

There are always two sides to every story, some say three, so I don't blame adult children for the estrangement, because although there are no perfect parents, there are bad parents. In circumstances of emotional, or sexual abuse, it may not be healthy or safe for the adult child, or their children, to be around their parent. In this case, an adult child cutting off a parent might be the only option, but what about the parent who did not do these things? What about the parents who tried their best to raise their children, protect them and provide for them?

The Root of Adult Child Parent Estrangement

Doctors and therapists have their beliefs as to why there is a division in the family, such as divorce, family dynamics, addiction, money, mental illness, abuse (physical, mental, emotional, and sexual), and I agree with them. However, these are merely symptoms of something much deeper and cynical. When I hear the stories, and the reasonings from parents behind the estrangement from their children, what I hear just doesn't merit the level of anger, animosity, abandonment, and the rejection they are receiving from their adult child. It just doesn't make sense.

This is why I believe family estrangement, and particularly adult child parent estrangement, is spiritual. It's like something evil has been unleashed on the earth to tear down families and steal our sons and daughters, and it has. Its name is Satan. It doesn't matter what you call him: Satan, Lucifer, Ole Louie, or the devil, he is far more sinister and diabolical than any pointed eared, pointed tale, pitchfork carrying cartoon character. He is real, and his primary goal is to steal, kill, and destroy you and your family.

Aside from the gift of His own Son, the family is God's greatest gift to mankind. When God instituted marriage and family, He had a beautiful eternal plan in mind, and He has given us His plan for what families should be. His desire is for us to walk with Him as His children, reflecting His nature and character.

Marriage is where God intends the family to thrive, and experience His love, and learn how to love others. In God's plan, the love between the husband and wife is a model of Christ's passionate love and devotion to His bride (Genesis 2:18, Ephesians 5:22-32). In the womb, God's plan continues, and flourishes. This is God's original design for marriage and family.

As beautiful and as perfect as God made the family to be, because of Adam and Eve's sin, we now live in a fallen world. Instead of healthy and thriving, many family relationships are difficult and toxic. God's plan for marriage is being heavily attacked today, but what many don't see is that the attack is led by Satan. He hates that a husband and wife can cleave to one another in God. His plan is to divide the family, then conquer each member.

Division is a tactic Satan uses to destroy from within. His first act of division was to divide the angels in heaven. Satan wanted to be like God, and he convinced one third of the angels of heaven to help him overthrow God, and there was a war in heaven. Of course, God and the remaining angels won, and Satan was thrown out of heaven, down to the earth, and the angels to hell (Isaiah 14:4–17; Isaiah 14:15; Ezekiel 28:16-17; 2 Peter 2:4).

Then, as soon as God created Adam and Eve, Satan came to divide them. When they sinned, they had no idea of the extent of pain and suffering that would come because of it. Like our first parents, we don't know the pain and suffering behind our sin until we are faced with the consequences. When God confronted Adam about his sin, he immediately blamed his wife, Eve, and God. He said, *"the woman whom you gave to be with me, she gave me fruit of the tree, and I ate"* (Genesis 3:12).

Adam's blaming God and then Eve, was the first divisive act in the family institution. The next divisive act showed up in their offspring, Cain and Abel. They had a troubled relationship that ended with Cain killing his younger brother. Adam and Eve's sin allowed division to be embedded in every family after that. Today, Satan and his demons continue to wage war against God by promoting division between God and humanity.

God's plan was completed before the foundation of the world, so no matter what he does, Satan's strength and plots will never prevail against faithful believers in Christ who will stand and believe God and His Word (Ephesians 1:4). The fight has already been won. I remind you that God is a God of unity, relationship, and love. God has given us the weapons to destroy the spirit of disunity. It is the weapon of prayer. Start by binding the spirit of disunity within your family (Matthew 16:19, Matthew 18:18). Then, ask God to bring the spirit of unity in your family. You can pray something like:

In the name of Jesus, I bind the spirit of disunity from my family and cast you out! Father God, thank You for binding the spirit of disunity from my family. I ask You to let the spirit of unity, and love reign in my family. Amen.

When Adam and Eve sinned, it was Satan's attempt to thwart God's plan for the family. He succeeded in causing them to disobey God, but he did not thwart God's plan. God had a contingency plan in place from the foundation of the world. His name is Jesus Christ (1 Peter 1:18-21). When they sinned, God pronounced a curse on Satan, which he has been retaliating against ever since.

"And the Lord God said unto the serpent, Because thou hast done this, thou art cursed above all cattle, and above every beast of the field; upon thy belly shalt thou go, and dust shalt thou eat all the days of thy life: And I will put enmity between thee and the woman, and between thy seed and her seed; it shall bruise thy head, and thou shalt bruise his heel."
–Genesis 3:14-15 KJV

In these words, God was telling Satan that Jesus would bruise his head by conquering sin and death; and He would make redemption available to mankind. He would also allow Satan to bruise Jesus' heel by influencing men to kill Him on the cross. This was necessary because without the shedding of blood, there is no remission of sin. So, God used Satan to save mankind, and to bring Satan's diabolical plan to naught (1 Timothy 4:10). Isn't God amazing?

Walking In Truth

"Search me, O God, and know my heart! Try me and know my thoughts! And see if there be any grievous way in me, and lead me in the way everlasting!" – Psalm 139:23-24

Self-examination is a crucial part of our spiritual growth, and a necessary part of healing the relationship between you and your child. Parents, we may have played a bigger part in the estrangement in our family than we realize. You may not like it, or want to admit it, but there may be some things you did that you may have forgotten, or that your kids saw differently than what you meant by it.

Because of generational differences, what we view as appropriate parenting behavior may be different from what our children see as appropriate. So, we may not agree with our estranged children about what went wrong. It is easy to deceive ourselves into thinking we are better, smarter, and more ethical than we really are. Proverbs 21:2 says, "Every way of a man is right in his own eyes: but the LORD pondereth the hearts."

I did things differently, raising my children, from what I was accustomed to when I was coming up. When my children had children, I noticed that they did things differently with their children than I did with them. What we regarded as normal behavior may be regarded as abusive or neglectful by our children.

One day, I said to my therapist, "I don't discount that they had a hard time dealing with me financially struggling, and us moving a lot when they were coming up, but they didn't really know about hard times." What they went through was nothing compared to what I endured as a child. I did my best to make sure they did not experience any of that." I didn't say this to compare. I really didn't understand how they could be so angry.

She said, "Angeline, what is a big thing for you is different from what is a big thing for them. Because they didn't experience the abuse and molestation you did, doesn't mean what they experienced didn't affect them just as much." She opened my eyes and helped me understand what they were saying and feeling. I apologized to them, but they were not ready to release the anger.

Making Amends

We may not know how our children perceive events that occurred when they were growing up. Remember when I said my youngest son told me that he had always been ashamed of me. I did not know that. My oldest son said I was never there for them. Even though I didn't agree with him, I had to hear him out, acknowledge what he said, and ask for forgiveness.

Scripture tells us,

Confess your trespasses to one another, and pray for one another, that you may be healed. —James 5:16

If it is possible, as much as depends on you, live peaceably with all men. —Romans 12:18

These Scriptures can clearly apply to our relationships with our adult children as well as other people. We should try to maintain peace with everyone if it is at all possible. When we are aware that we have wronged another person, the will of God is for us to go to them quickly and admit our sin and seek their forgiveness.

It is important to admit your errors when confronted with them. If your estranged child will talk with you, allow them to get out what's troubling them, and take responsibility for your part without getting defensive. Whether they accept it or not, sincerely apologize for anything wrong that you may have said or done.

Confessing your errors can soften their heart to be more receptive to forgiveness and reconciliation. Even if he or she is not ready to forgive, your sincere confession will keep your heart clean, and display humility, which can lead to reconciliation later. Denying your faults is prideful, makes you unrepentant, and will more than likely prolong your family's healing.

"Pride goes before destruction, and a haughty spirit before a fall. Better to be of a humble spirit with the lowly, than to divide the spoil with the proud."
– Proverbs 16:18 (NIV)

Pride makes us vulnerable to destruction. God resists the proud, but gives grace to the humble (James 4:6). Remember, apologies not accompanied by change are worthless. 2nd Corinthians 13:5 says, we should examine ourselves, to see whether we are in the faith. Paul is talking about examining whether we are living as God wants us to live. This should include examining whether we have done things unintentionally to cause a rift in the family as well.

"Fathers, do not provoke your children to anger by the way you treat them. Rather, bring them up with the discipline and instruction that comes from the Lord." – Ephesians 6:4

We know that children don't come with an instruction manual, so we were bound to make some mistakes, and we probably did do some provoking. This is why we should spend some time with God and allow Him to assist us in examining our relationship with our children. He was there, and He knows how to lovingly point out anything that needs to be dealt with.

Self-examination is not about beating yourself up about your mistakes, your past, or even blaming yourself. Satan and your kids do enough of that. It is about acknowledging, repenting, forgiving, healing, and moving on. Get in a quiet place with God, fast and pray, and have an intimate discussion with Him about your experiences and emotions, then and now, so He can heal you.

I have learned that in order to move forward in life, we must face and accept what is, and learn from our mistakes. I said earlier that while raising my kids, I made some decisions that I would probably do differently if given the chance, and some I wouldn't change at all. Before salvation, I did things that people who don't have a relationship with God do. Many of those things I would change.

After salvation, I still did some things, I should not have done. Many of those things I would also change. But then again, I wouldn't be who I am today without those things. They have made me stronger, and helped me minister to many people. So, just like Judas was necessary, the things we went through were necessary as well.

In every relationship, there will be differences of opinion and conflict. No one likes to be wrongly accused, and most people don't want to apologize for something they did not do. Being asked to apologize when you feel you've done nothing wrong might make you angry or defensive, but becoming angry and defensive will not help the situation.

Apologizing is not an admission of guilt, but an act of humility and an act of love. Sometimes it's just better to apologize even when you're right, for the sake of maintaining peace. You don't have to fight to prove yourself right in eve-ry instance. God knows the truth. Choose the relationship with your child over being right. Remember what 1st Corinthians 13:4-7 says?

"Love is patient and kind; love does not envy or boast; it is not arrogant or rude. It does not insist on its own way; it is not irritable or resentful; it does not rejoice at wrongdoing, but rejoices with the truth. Love bears all things, believes all things, hopes all things, endures all things."

Words like "but," and "if" in apologies makes it sound like you are blaming them, or trying to justify your actions. Just listen and apologize, even if you disagree. Be the peacemaker.

"Strive for peace with everyone, and for the holiness without which no one will see the Lord. See to it that no one fails to obtain the grace of God; that no "root of bitterness" springs up and causes trouble, and by it many become defiled." – Hebrews 12:14-15 ESV

Maintain hope by speaking and praying God's

Word over them. Speaking and praying God's Word over any situation that I face brings me comfort and helps me to stand in faith until God works everything out. Isaiah 49:16 which says, *"See, I have engraved you on the palms of my hands; your walls are ever before me"* is very encouraging for me. What a comfort to know that me and my sons' names are engraved in the hand of Jesus and ever before Him. Psalm 139 is another encouraging Scripture that I personalize and pray for them.

Here is an example of how you can personalize this passage:

Lord God, You know my sons. You know when they sit down and when they rise. You discern their thoughts from afar. You are acquainted with all their ways. Where shall they go from your Spirit? Or flee from your presence? Wherever they go, You are there! I praise you, for they are fearfully and wonderfully made. Father, help them to listen to what You say, and to treasure Your commands. Instruct them in the way of wisdom and lead them in the way everlasting. In Jesus' name I pray.

When you pray, believe God heard you and will answer. It may take some time, but praise God and continue to praise Him for restoring your family, and thank God for the answer.

Forgiveness Is Necessary

Peter says in 1st Peter 5:8, *"Your adversary, the devil, walks about like a roaring lion, seeking whom he may devour."* Notice Peter refers to the devil as "your" adversary. That makes it personal. His assaults are personal. Satan has several weapons that he uses in his quest to destroy mankind, and unforgiveness is one of Satan's most effective weapons of destruction. His biggest targets are the family and the church, so you will find that most of the offense comes from family and unconverted church members. Offense is an open door for unforgiveness.

Apologizing is not an admission of guilt, but an act of humility and an act of love.

Unforgiveness is rooted in a spirit of pride, and it keeps us in bondage to sin. It makes no allowance for error, or the weakness of others. It demands punishment, and does not rest until it either destroys its victim, or until it is conquered and put down. Unforgiveness has an assignment from Satan to keep replaying hurtful memories to remind you of bad things that happened to you.

Unforgiveness must be dealt with. It is dangerous because when you refuse to forgive others, the unresolved anger is an open door for a satanic or ungodly stronghold to be formed in your heart and mind. A stronghold is a walled-up place, or fortress, built to keep something out. That wall or stronghold can be built with blocks of rejection, offense, fear, depression, anger, addiction, bitterness, pride, unforgiveness and more. Satan and his demonic forces are skilled at using the words and actions of others to harden our heart and build strongholds where they can dwell or hide in.

They may lie dormant until we are in a vulnerable or weakened state and, from that fortified stronghold, launch an attack on our heart and mind. Jesus taught on the dangers of harboring unforgiveness, and instructed His followers on how to protect themselves against it. He said God will not forgive us if we choose not to forgive others (Matthew 6:14-15). Human nature, or the flesh, does not like to forgive.

Many people go beyond anger, and want to get

even, and get revenge. When they are offended or emotionally wounded, they think if I forgive the person, they will just hurt me again. They think holding on to the anger and not forgiving punishes the one who offended them. This is different from not trusting the person again. We don't ever have to trust them again, but we do have to forgive them.

Some people find the offense so heinous that they are unable to forgive. None of this is true. All things are possible with God (Matthew 19:26). Sadly, when an unforgiving person realizes that they are the ones who are hurt the most, they have been engulfed with the destructive results of unforgiveness.

Unforgiveness grieves the Holy Spirit. Ephesians 4:30-32 says bitterness, anger, wrath, quarreling, slander, and hatred grieve the Holy Spirit of God. Looking at the behaviors that grieve the Holy Spirit: Were some or all of these behaviors present prior to the separation between you and your child?

Many illnesses are related to unforgiveness. In fact, unforgiveness is classified in medical books as a disease. According to the article "The Deadly Consequences of Unforgiveness" forgiveness therapy is an integral part of treatment at Cancer Treatment Centers of America.[1]

Dr. Michael Barry, a pastor and the author of the book, *The Forgiveness Project* states "Of all cancer patients, 61 percent have forgiveness issues, and of those, more than half are severe. Harboring these negative emotions, this anger and hatred, creates a state of chronic anxiety. Chronic anxiety produces excess adrenaline and cortisol, which deplete the production of natural killer cells, which is your body's foot soldier in the fight against cancer," he explained. Forgiveness is powerful. People have been healed of sickness and infirmity instantly once unforgiveness has been taken care of spiritually.

People who hold unforgiveness in their heart are not right with God, no matter what Satan has deceived them into believing. No matter how much they pretend to be happy, they lack true joy and peace in their life. They are critical and judgmental of the people around them, especially of those closest to them. They blame their unhappiness on others, but the real problem lies in the fact that they are

---

[1] (*CBN News Jun 22, 2015, www1.cbn.com*)

out of fellowship with the Lord. This is why forgiveness is not optional. These scriptures talk about unforgiveness and why we need to forgive:

Proverbs 24:17-18: *"Do not rejoice when your enemy falls, and do not let your heart be glad when he stumbles; lest the Lord see it, and it displease Him, and He turn away His wrath from him."*

Romans 12:20-21: *"Therefore "If your enemy is hungry, feed him; if he is thirsty, give him a drink; for in so doing, you will heap coals of fire on his head." Do not be overcome by evil, but overcome evil with good."*

Matthew 5:39-42: *"But I say to you, Do not resist the one who is evil. But if anyone slaps you on the right cheek, turn to him the other also. And if anyone would sue you and take your tunic, let him have your cloak as well. And if anyone forces you to go one mile, go with him two miles. Give to the one who begs from you, and do not refuse the one who would borrow from you."*

Matthew 5:43-46: *"You have heard that it was said, 'You shall love your neighbor and hate your enemy.' But I say to you, Love your enemies and pray for* *those who persecute you, so that you may be sons of your Father who is in heaven. For he makes his sun rise on the evil and on the good, and sends rain on the just and on the unjust. For if you love those who love you, what reward do you have? Do not even the tax collectors do the same?"*

Hebrews 12:15 in the Passion Translation cautions us to, *"Watch over each other to make sure that no one misses the revelation of God's grace. And make sure no one lives with a root of bitterness sprouting within them, which will only cause trouble and poison the hearts of many."*

1st John 3:15 warns, *"Anyone who hates a brother or sister is a murderer, and you know that no murderer has eternal life residing in him."*

Can you see how destructive unforgiveness is, and why forgiving those who have hurt us is so important? Forgiveness is not a one time act. It is a way of thinking and a way of living. Forgiveness is a heart issue, but it is not a feeling or an emotion. You don't have to feel all mushy and gooey to be forgiving, so don't wait for those emotions to appear before you forgive someone.

Forgiveness is a decision to release the person who hurt, or betrayed you. It is letting go of resentment toward that person, and releasing the right to be bitter, and the right to get even. Dr. Martin Luther King, Jr. said, *"Forgiveness is not an occasional act, it is a constant attitude."* While He was dying on the cross Jesus said, *"Father, forgive them for they know not what they do!"*

Jesus understands human weakness, and He knows that without the help of the Holy Spirit and His grace, it is really impossible to truly forgive. Psalm 34:18 says, *"The LORD is close to the brokenhearted and saves those who are crushed in spirit."* In our weakness, His strength is made perfect (2 Corinthians 12:9). *"My grace is sufficient,"* said the Lord.

Recognize that the same devil who is trying to destroy you is trying to destroy your offender. They are being used by Satan in his attempt to destroy all concerned, including them. They may recognize this, and want to be free of what they are experiencing, but don't know how to get free. God may want to use you to help both of you get free. Truly forgiving an offender is to love them enough to pray for them.

Forgiveness is essential in repairing relationships. I want a relationship with my sons, so over the years, I have listened to my sons' complaints and tried to understand why they feel the way they do about me (real or perceived). I've tried not to deny their views, and I have sincerely apologized over and over for all that they continuously bring to my attention. However, they have not accepted my apology, so we keep going in circles.

As long as unforgiveness is present, healing and restoration of the relationship will be impossible. At this point, what do you do? You take your focus off them and the situation, give them to God, and work on letting God heal you. *"Commit thy way unto the Lord; trust also in Him; and he shall bring it to pass"* (Psalm 37:5). As devastating as adult child parent estrangement is, God can use it for good.

In the meantime, while you are waiting for God to bring your family back together, let God heal you. If you want the relationship between you and your child restored, you have got to let go of them, and any unforgiveness you may be holding against your child or anyone else. Release it now. Also, it is important to forgive yourself, too. If you have asked God to forgive you of your sins with a sincere heart, it is done.

In the section *Scriptures and Prayers* is a prayer that you can pray for help to be set free from offense, bitterness, and unforgiveness.

Rejection From The Womb

"For I know the plans I have for you," says the Lord. "They are plans for good and not for disaster, to give you a future and a hope." – Jeremiah 29:11

God created humans to be social beings, to desire love and acceptance. He gave us the family as one of the places where we can receive the love and acceptance we desire. One of the greatest gifts a parent can give their child is a sense of being wanted and accepted. Unfortunately, many people suffer from a sense of being unwanted or rejected by the people around them. Rejection is at the root of the high suicide rate, and the high number of people suffering from depression. All of this is an indication that rejection is another one of Satan's most effective and common tools that he uses to destroy the family unit.

The definition of rejection is to cast aside, throw away, dislike, refuse to accept, look down upon with disdain, and discard something as being worthless. It can be directed towards a person or a thing. Rejection, like every other weapon Satan uses against us, has an assignment. Its assignment is to separate us from love and distort our image of God as a loving heavenly Father. Its goal is to weaken and prevent harmonious relationships between husband and wife, children, parents, and family members.

As long as unforgiveness is present, healing and restoration of the relationship will be impossible.

Rejection is like a tree with a bitter root. It can only produce bitter fruit. Rejection does not discriminate. It attaches itself to people of any age, young or old, rich, or poor, black, or white, well-educated or uneducated. It can be deeply rooted and woven into their identities before, during, and after birth. It destroys self-esteem and prevents us from carrying out our God-given purposes in life. It causes people to feel and regard others as unacceptable, of no value, doesn't belong, unwanted, can't fit in, and unloved. These are the feelings that the conversations my sons left me with when we talked.

As I continued to pray about what caused the estrangement within my family and other families, I heard the words *"rejected from the womb."* Immediately, I was reminded of the events that happened during each of my pregnancies. I won't go into the details here because I haven't discussed any negatives with my children about what occurred during my pregnancy with them. I never wanted them to feel that they were a mistake, unwanted or unloved. However, from what they've said to me, this ended up being their feelings, anyway. As God opened my understanding about rejection from the womb, so much of what was happening began to make sense.

When I researched the subject, I found that numerous studies have been done showing that babies can hear what is being said around them while in the womb. They can taste the foods that their mother eats. They can feel love, lack of love, and rejection from their mother, father, siblings, and those around them. They learn their father's and mother's voices. They react to what's going on around them while in the womb, and they experience emotions such as anxiety, stress, sadness, and more.

> **Rejection's assignment is to separate us from love and distort our image of God as a loving heavenly Father.**

Rarely is there a single cause for rejection. There are many other ways strongholds are built. Rejection in the womb is but one way they start. Most people are wounded in many ways. Each new wound adds to the pain and hurt which already exists. Over time, as the child grows, the enemy will use the negative things the child hears and feels to build strongholds in their mind.

Remember, a stronghold is a walled-up place, or fortress in the heart and mind of a person made up of twisted truths, ungodly beliefs, and lies. These lies create depression, anxiety, doubt, and even addiction. Does all this sound farfetched to you? Let's take a look at the parable Jesus told in Matthew Chapter 13,

> *"[24] Another parable He put forth to them, saying: "The kingdom of heaven is like a man who sowed good seed in his field; [25] but while men slept, his enemy came and sowed tares among the wheat and went his way. [26] But when the grain had sprouted*

and produced a crop, then the tares also appeared. ^{27} So the servants of the owner came and said to him, 'Sir, did you not sow good seed in your field? How then does it have tares?' ^{28} He said to them, 'An enemy has done this.' The servants said to him, 'Do you want us then to go and gather them up?'" —Matthew 13:24-28

Most people are so focused on what they see with their physical eyes, they do not account for the unseen. I really want you to grab hold of what I'm saying. You need to know and understand that there is a great war over the life and conception of children. The enemy Jesus is talking about is Satan. Jesus said the enemy came at night while the servants were asleep. He snuck in and sowed weeds in their field.

That is what Satan is doing today. He sneaks around looking for people who are not on the alert, people who are helpless and vulnerable, no matter their age or status (1 Peter 5:8). When he finds one, he whispers his ungodly thoughts (seeds) into their heart to plant doubt, self-pity, pride, unforgiveness, hate, anger, bitterness, discord, insecurity, discontentment, and more in their heart. The goal is to get us and our children to put love of self ahead of love for God and one another.

Notice that the servants didn't realize what the enemy had done until the weeds started showing up. The spirit of rejection is one of Satan's favorite tools to use. He is patient, but he does not wait very long to make his move. He may even start at conception, and work for years against us.

Does it seem like one day your beautiful child went to sleep and woke up as someone else? The Scripture says that over time, the weeds began to sprout up along with the wheat. Satan does the same thing in families. He sneaks in and, over time, works to undermine and destroy your family. You name it, he tries it. He may entice the husband or wife to be unfaithful to their covenant of marriage.

He may encourage one or both of them to put too much emphasis on their career, or spend too much time pursuing things. He might plant seeds of doubt in the husband's or the wife's mind about their choice to marry. He may convince the father, or the mother, that they would be better off if they just left the family. He might introduce envy, jealousy, dishonesty, or rebellion amongst the kids. The possibilities of his tactics are endless, and you can be sure that he is the master of them all.

No matter what has happened in your family, or your child, God can turn things around. God is answering the cry of your heart right now by shedding light on the lies and tactics that have come to sabotage your family. The gates hell shall not prevail! The seed of the righteous shall be delivered.

There are many actions that may cause rejection to form in your child while in the womb. Not every parent is excited by the news that they are expecting a child. The news of conception is the easiest place for the spirit of rejection to begin its work. Think back. What were your thoughts when you learned you were pregnant with your estranged child? What was going on in your life? Was your baby a surprise?

Did you try to abort, or talk about aborting, or putting the child up for adoption? Did you have resentment because of the pregnancy? Did you or the father want one sex and got the other? Was the pregnancy the result of a one-night stand, the act of adultery, or rape? Were you a teen mom and felt unprepared to be a mother? Was there some other trauma or chaos that occurred around the pregnancy?

The more I learned, the more I saw that I have been dealing with a spirit of rejection my entire life. I believe a seed of rejection was planted in me in my mother's womb, and watered as I grew up. My dad was an angry man, and he was abusive to my mother. The earliest memory I have of my parents is watching my dad being hauled off in handcuffs after him and my mother had a fight over how she was treating me. When he and my mother split up, he took me from her and dropped me off on his mother's doorstep. I don't think she was pleased with his decision because she was very abusive to me, emotionally and physically.

Everyone knew I was being abused, but no one helped me. One of my cousins said they thought she didn't like girls because she was mean to all her granddaughters. Her mother was born a slave, and she grew up in a small town in Georgia. So maybe her way of raising kids was to be a hard taskmaster. My dad was a heroin addict, so he was rarely there. I felt unloved and unwanted. One thing my grandmother did do was send me to the church down the street on Sundays. I walked there every Sunday, and

I learned a little about God. Writing letters and poetry to God became my escape. Even though I was in the midst of such abuse, God had His hand on me.

One story in the Bible that always encourages me is found in Mark 4:35-41. Jesus and His disciples were in a boat headed to the other side of the sea. As they were crossing over, a storm rose. The lesson I get from the story is that even though Jesus was in the boat with them, a storm still rose. Even though they didn't fully trust Jesus, He rose and calmed the storm. Jesus knew the storm would come when He said, *"Let us go to the other side."*

Notice that the servants didn't realize what the enemy had done until the weeds started showing up. The spirit of rejection is one of Satan's favorite tools to use. He is patient, but he does not wait very long to make his move. He may even start at conception, and work for years against us. Does it seem like one day your beautiful child went to sleep and woke up as someone else? The Scripture says that over time, the weeds began to sprout up along with the wheat. Satan does the same thing in families. He sneaks in and, over time, works to undermine and destroy your family. You name it, he tries it.

He may entice the husband or wife to be unfaithful to their covenant of marriage. He may encourage one or both of them to put too much emphasis on their career, or spend too much time pursuing things. He might plant seeds of doubt in the husband's or the wife's mind about their choice to marry.

He may convince the father, or the mother, that they would be better off if they just left the family. He might introduce envy, jealousy, dishonesty, or rebellion amongst the kids. The possibilities of his tactics are endless, and you can be sure that he is the master of them all.

The Lord has not promised that we won't have trouble in life. In fact, He has told us to expect trouble (John 16:33). What He has promised is that He will be with us in the storm. If we have accepted Him as Lord and Savior, He will never leave us alone when we are in the midst of trouble.

> *"Do not be afraid or discouraged, for the LORD will personally go ahead of you. He will be with you; he will neither fail you nor abandon you." – Deuteronomy 31:8 NLT*
>
> *"God blesses those who patiently endure testing and*

temptation. Afterward they will receive the crown of life that God has promised to those who love him." – James 1:12 NLT

If Jesus was able to rescue the apostles from the storm, He is also able to rescue us from the storms we face. He has calmed so many storms in my life, and I know He will do the same for you.

I also saw that my children were dealing with the spirit of rejection, too. God revealed this was the root of our estrangement, and it may be the root of estrangement in your family. Does your child, or you, struggle with rejection?

Seeds always bear some type of fruit. Rejection has a lot of fruit, which can widely vary from one person to another. Some of the common symptoms of rejection include:

- Inability to receive love and to love others.
- Excessive shyness and feeling inferior.
- Constant feelings of inadequacy and inferiority.
- Self-pity, feeling bad for being all alone.
- Fear of rejection, always in a performance mode, trying to please others.
- The tendency to reject others, before they reject

you.

- Lack of ability to be corrected or receive constructive criticism.
- Critical of self and others.
- Inability to trust and suspicious of others.
- Constantly comparing yourself to others.
- Feelings of worthlessness, insecurity, withdrawal, and hopelessness.
- Giving off a sense of superiority.
- Opinionated personality and the need to be right all the time.

Do you recognize any of these in your child, or in you? It's time for this to stop! Jesus came to set the captives free. The Bible teaches us that God wants us all to be uprooted from Satan's kingdom and then replanted into God's kingdom. This is what God wants to do with your child and you. He not only wants us to be replanted, but we are to become rooted and grounded in the love of God. We can walk in victory despite the spiritual battle in our family.

If you realize you have been used to cause

rejection in your child, ask God for forgiveness, and then ask Him to help you reach out to your child, and bring forgiveness. If your child is unwilling to talk with you, write them a letter, or email. Acknowledge that you understand why they feel the way they do, and apologize for the hurt that you have caused them. Keep it simple. Apologize and let them know you love and miss them and would like to reconnect when they are ready. Always pray, believing as you pray that God will turn things around.

In the section *Scriptures and Prayers* is a prayer that you can pray for healing from rejection.

Guilt, Shame, and Condemnation

"I, even I, am He who blots out your transgressions for My own sake; and I will not remember your sins."
– Isaiah 43:25

Guilt

Guilt and shame are common emotions in adult child parents' estranged relationships. Guilt is about behavior, what we've done or failed to do, and it is about conviction and confession. Guilt is usually accompanied by thoughts of "if only I had." However, guilt is not always a bad thing. It can actually be a signal that there is something we need to deal with, especially when we have hurt someone.

The proper response when we have hurt someone is to confess our error, apologize, and then move on, leaving the guilt behind (1 John 1:9). If you don't have remorse when you have hurt someone, this is also a signal of something in your heart that needs to be dealt with.

Shame

Shame comes from a negative belief about who you are. Shame condemns you and tells you that there is something deeply wrong with you. It convinces you that you are inadequate and not enough, and that others are looking at you in a bad way. Shame makes you feel embarrassed and dirty, like the only way to deal with your mistakes and failure is to run away and hide from people and from God. If shame can convince you that these things are true, then shame decides for you who you are.

Satan uses shame to make you think you are condemned by God. After Adam and Eve sinned, they were ashamed of what they had done, and they felt condemned, so they hid in fear. When God approached them, instead of confessing their sin and releasing the guilt, they passed blame. As mentioned earlier, Adam blamed God, and Eve, and Eve blamed the Serpent (Satan). Shame also causes people to build walls of protection and lash out at others to prevent people from seeing who they really are. Shame is definitely something you want to get rid of.

Condemnation

Condemnation is the accusing voice of our personal adversary, Satan telling us how bad we are, that God is going to get us for the bad things we've said and done, that we are unworthy of God's love, mercy, and forgiveness. Condemnation and unforgiveness have the same assignment, which is to get us to re-live the past. They attempt to recycle painful memories, events, and sin that we have committed, or that have been committed against us to keep us in a cycle of defeat and oppression. Don't allow Satan to draw you into rehearsing recycling negative thinking. Cast down those thoughts and imaginations. Ask the Holy Ghost to help you and He will.

Reaping What You Sow

Satan will even twist God's Word to try to get you to accept his lies, like he did in the Garden with Eve. Remember, he has no new tricks. One passage of Scripture that works particularly well for him to bring shame and condemnation is Galatians 6:7, which says, *"Whatever a man sows, that he will also reap."*

When you have done something wrong, he will bombard you with thoughts like, "You must take responsibility and pay for what you have done," or "God is causing you to reap what you've sown." This is why it is so important to study the Word of God with the Holy Spirit, and get an understanding for yourself. Always pray and ask God to give you understanding before you study His Word.

Satan tried to tell me that the estrangement between me and my sons was me reaping what I'd sown with my mother. My mother and I did not have a close relationship. A few days short of my thirteenth birthday, I ran away from my dad's mother to live with my mother. When I got there, I endured a lot of trauma because of the lifestyle that she lived. After one incident, I'd had enough. I moved and didn't let anyone in the family know where I was. I just could not handle what was going on anymore, and I wanted better for my kids.

One day, my oldest son came home from school

and said a boy in his third-grade class had tried to make him smoke marijuana. Even as a little girl, I never wanted to live in Miami, so that day I made the decision that I would leave. I talked with the guy I was dating, and a female friend who was escaping an abusive relationship. He had some friends in Atlanta who were buying and flipping houses, and he arranged to do some carpentry work in exchange for us living there until we got settled. So, we all decided on Atlanta, Georgia.

We arrived in Atlanta on February 8th, 1988. We stayed in his friend's house on Edgewood Avenue. The house wasn't in the best shape, but it was a roof over our heads until we could get settled. I started working at a print shop two days later. Within two months, we all separated, and I have not seen them since. I have always believed it was the hand of God that led me to leave Miami. I believe God orchestrated the move with what I thought was their support because I did not have the courage to make the move with three small kids alone. There were many rumors and lies being spread about me and my children back in Miami by my siblings and even my mother. I did not feel comfortable going back. I was a single parent, and there were a lot of struggles, but I always felt this was the best decision for me and my kids.

It is true, if we sow bad things, we will reap bad things (Proverbs 22:8). It is also true, *if we confess our sins, He [God] is faithful and just to forgive us our sins, and to cleanse us from all unrighteousness* (1 John 1:9). Satan has convinced many people that God is out to get them when they go through hard times. They believe that God is punishing them for their mistakes and sins. I've heard pastors preach that God punishes Believers for their sins, and that He punishes people when they leave their local church for another. This belief and teaching contradict the finished works of Christ.

Always forgive yourself. Don't allow guilt to consume you. Give peace!

I want you to know and understand that God is not out to get us. If He were, He would have gotten us a long time ago. We have certainly given Him plenty of reasons to wipe us all out. Besides, if God was out to get us, He never would have sent Jesus to the cross to bear His wrath in our place. Jesus took

God's wrath upon Himself (Isaiah 53:10). The moment we believe in Jesus, all sins past, present, and future are forgiven, and we are seated with Christ in heaven (Hebrews 10:17-18, Ephesians 2:6-9).

"By God's will we have been purified and made holy once and for all through the sacrifice of the body of Jesus, the Messiah!" —Hebrews 10:10 TPT

As a child of God, no matter how many mistakes you make, you are not condemned. The Bible says, "*There is therefore now no condemnation to those who are in Christ Jesus, who do not walk according to the flesh, but according to the Spirit*" (Romans 8:1).

When a Believer experiences the consequences of sin, it is not because they are under God's wrath, or being condemned by God. It is because we live in a fallen world. Every person will experience some of sin's consequences because we are all children of Adam (Romans 5:12). We all get sick and grow old, and we will all eventually die physically. Saved or unsaved, there's no avoiding the consequences of the original sin.

Then there are the consequences of man's law. For instance, if you steal something, you may get caught and have to face the consequences of stealing. I have a friend whose son was murdered. As hard as it was to do, she forgave the man who killed her son, but that man still received a hefty prison sentence for the murder.

Then there is God's discipline, which some mistake as punishment. Sometimes God will allow us to bear the consequences of our actions so that we will change the negative behavior. There is no denying that we learn from our mistakes when we bear the consequences of them. Proverbs 22:8 says, *"whoever sows injustice reaps calamity, and the rod they wield in fury will be broken."* However even then, there is opportunity for repentance and forgiveness.

> *"Do not remember the former things, Nor con-sider the things of old. Behold, I will do a new thing, Now it shall spring forth; Shall you not know it? I will even make a road in the wilderness, and rivers in the desert." –Isaiah 43:18-19*

Refuse to accept the enemy's lies of condemnation. We all make mistakes. We all fail family members. We all fail friends. We all fail ourselves, and we all fail God. Fear and condemnation are not from

God. God is love! Your adult child, and others, may be holding things against you, but God is not. God promises in Hebrews 8:12, *"For I will be merciful to their unrighteousness, and their sins and their lawless deeds I will remember no more."*

Once we have acknowledged our errors to our children, asked for forgiveness and done our best to make amends, we have done what God requires of us. It is up to them to accept the apology, or to reject it. Once you have repented and asked God to forgive you, believe that He has forgiven you! If God has forgiven you, no one has the right to bring up your past mistakes and sins! Neither Satan, your family, your friends, and not even you have a right to condemn you, after God has forgiven you!!

Ask and you shall receive! Ask God to heal and restore your family.

Many times, after we repent, and know that God has forgiven us, we do not forgive ourselves! Always forgive yourself. Don't let guilt consume you. Give peace a chance in your heart. When you do not forgive yourself, Satan can attack you with thoughts of self-condemnation. If you are struggling with feeling condemned, I urge you to run to Jesus and the Word of God. Ask the Holy Spirit to illuminate His Word to you, and take your burdens to the Lord in prayer.

Stay Alert

"Be sober, be vigilant; because your adversary the devil walks about like a roaring lion, seeking whom he may devour." –1 Peter 5:8

While writing this book, I allowed my sister to move into my home. I cannot stress enough how important it is to seek God and godly counsel before making decisions that will affect your life and your peace. Satan, your personal adversary, is diabolical and very crafty. He knows every button to push to get you to take your focus off of who you are in Christ, and start talking, walking, and acting out his plan of destruction for you.

Almost immediately after she moved in, things became strained in my home. Everything I said and did seemed to annoy her. I started walking around on pins and needles, not wanting to talk in my own home to keep peace. I sensed that she was ready to go back to Miami, and since she had come up with an elaborate story to get help to leave, she had to come up with another elaborate story to get help to go back.

The strife was increasing, and peace had left my home. One night, I could not sleep, and I got up and walked through my house, and anointed it with oil, prayed in the spirit, and declared the Word of God until I felt a breakthrough. I spoke directly to Satan and every demon I sensed that had entered my house and cast them out of my home. The next day, I heard her on the phone telling someone that I was crazy and that I was abusing her, and making other false accusations about me. For the next few days, the tensions got worse.

She called my oldest son, who was already saying all manner of evil to me, and about me, and told him her lies too. He called me, and without even asking what happened, he started yelling at me, accusing me of the things she said. He called my youngest son and told him I was a drug addict on crack. I knew that lie came from her because she told me she remembered me using crack with my mother, which never happened.

I was amazed that she had no problem telling these lies with a straight face. Enlisting my sons started even more drama. She even threatened to call my pastors because they didn't know that I was not the person they thought I was, and she needed to tell them. She did call my Assistant Pastor, but she didn't answer and didn't return the call. I felt as if I was in a literal lion's den. Satan was mad, and he was using these three people to try to shame me and destroy my character. She just wanted a free ticket back home.

Now, I know that you can't fight spiritual things with flesh, but one day I'd had enough. I should have walked away and prayed. Before I knew it, I was drawn into an argument with her. I realized the accusations that were consistently being hurled at me by her were full of years of hatred and jealousy. When I walked away, I felt bad that I had allowed myself to be taken in by the enemy.

Holy Spirit showed me that I was dealing with the accuser of the brethren (Revelation 12:10). This was the same spirit that had attacked me through my sons, and it had to leave my home! If she didn't want to let it go, then she had to leave with it! I asked

God to forgive me for not seeking Him before allowing her to move into my home, and to forgive me for allowing myself to be drawn into an argument (Proverbs 3:5-7). I prayed and bound up that spirit (accuser of the brethren) and commanded it out of my house. Two days later, she was gone. I anointed my house, prayed, and welcomed peace back in.

"And I will give you the keys of the kingdom of heaven, and whatever you bind on earth will be bound in heaven, and whatever you loose on earth will be loosed in heaven." – Matthew 16:19

Again, I say to you that it is important to seek God, and godly counsel before making decisions that will affect your life, and your peace. The setup started when I got a phone call from her. She talked of committing suicide, and I opened my heart and my home to her, knowing that she can't stand me. I never asked God before doing so. This was a costly and powerful lesson to learn. If you find yourself having fallen for Satan's tricks, ask God to forgive you, and help you to stand and keep going. Don't allow condemnation and guilt to keep you bound up.

Breaking Generational Cycles

When God called Abraham and told him to leave his country, and his relatives, He made him a promise that would last throughout all generations. When He covenanted with Abraham, He covenanted with his offspring as well. This includes you (Galatians 3:29). He has covenanted with you concerning your family.

What if God has called you to bring salvation and deliverance to your family, and this is the reason you are enduring so much trouble in your family? This is something I have sensed for a very long time, concerning me and my family. When I left Florida to come to Atlanta with three small kids, I knew I was being called away. As time passes, and I draw closer to the Lord, I see that all the tribulation, including the estrangement from my sons, is Satan trying to steal our destiny.

Satan knows that when we, the children of God,

walk into a room, Christ walks in with us, and the atmosphere changes. Light shines in the midst of any darkness that is there. He knows that when we call on the name of Jesus, he and every demon must cease their activities and bow. So, he continues to do all he can to distract us, and make us doubt God, but with God's discernment, usually the opposite occurs. We trust God all the more.

Has God called you to bring salvation and deliverance to your family?

Through all the trials I have endured, my faith is being made stronger. I've learned about the tools God has given us and how to use them, and I teach others how to use them. So, you see, no weapon formed against us will prosper unless we allow it to do so. God is not going to override your authority or your will.

In the Book of Genesis, we see that God gave Adam authority in the Earth. When Adam relinquished his authority to Satan, God didn't stop him because He also gave Adam the right to choose to follow God, just as we have today. Jesus took bac what Adam lost. Now, through Jesus, Believers have been given the same authority in the earth. He has also given you the tools for victory in every situation—His Word.

Revelation of God's truth makes us free.

This is why I can firmly stand on what God has declared: the seed of the righteous shall be delivered. This is not to say that my other family members are not called into the Kingdom of God. They are, for the Bible says in 2nd Peter 3:9, *"The Lord is not willing that any should perish, but that all should come to repentance."*

When God saved you, His desire for salvation did not stop with you. God wants to heal your family starting with you. When we allow Him to, God uses us to break cycles in our bloodline. The Bible has several examples of God calling a person out to save families, for instance:

- Noah and his family. (Genesis 7:1)
- Abraham and his seed. (Genesis 17:5-7)
- Rahab and her family. (Joshua 6:17)

The Bible says in Romans 10:14, "How then will they call on him in whom they have not believed?

And how are they to believe in him of whom they have never heard? And how are they to hear without someone preaching?" One translation says, how can they hear without a preacher? The answer is, they can't.

Prayer and sharing the Gospel is crucial in the Earth today. Jesus said in Matthew 9:37-38, *"The harvest truly is plentiful, but the laborers are few. Therefore, pray the Lord of the harvest to send out laborers into His harvest."* Before my daughter left to go home with the Lord, she had a glimpse of heaven, and she said, "Mama, don't stop praying for our family."

> **"Greater is He that is in you than he that is in the world." With Christ, we will be victorious.**

Maybe you have tried ministering to your child and other members of your family, but they have turned a deaf ear to your voice. If they won't listen to you, there is someone that they will listen to. Somebody they will believe. Jesus said we can ask the Lord of The Harvest to send someone to our loved ones who they will listen to (Matthew 9:37-38). Continue to ask God to send laborers until they respond.

Stand on God's Word, and let God use you to stand in faith and pray, and declare His word over your family for their deliverance. In the words of my daughter, "don't stop praying for your family." God has a good plan for you, your children, and your family. Have the confidence in Him, that if you ask anything according to His will, He hears you and *has answered* your prayer (1 John 5:14). Again, it is not God's will for anyone to perish. Therefore, ask God to save your loved one.

Pull Down Strongholds That Pull You Down

When we are sick, the symptoms of the illness show on the surface, but the symptoms are not the cause. For instance, a sore throat, stuffy nose, and body aches are flu symptoms, but the flu virus is the root cause of the problem. So, it is with 99% of the problems we face in our life. When we are trying to fix something in our life, the symptoms are much easier to deal with than the root of the problem. However, until we deal with the root, the symptoms will just keep resurfacing. To be free of the issue, the best thing to do is find the root of the problem. Deal with the root and the symptoms will take care of themselves.

Remember, in Matthew Chapter 16 when Jesus shared with His disciples that He needed to go to Jerusalem and be killed, and be raised again on the third day? Scripture says, Peter rebuked Jesus, saying, *"Far be it from you, Lord! This shall never happen to you."* Jesus didn't rebuke Peter, He rebuked Satan saying, *"Get behind Me, Satan! You are an offense to Me, for you are not mindful of the things of God, but the things of men."* (Matthew 16:23).

Peter wasn't demon possessed, and I don't believe he meant to be an offense to Jesus either, but Satan did. Jesus knew that it was Satan who inspired Peter's statement, and Jesus went after the real source. I remind you that it is not your children, who must be dealt with, but Satan and his spiritual wickedness in high places" (Ephesians 6:13).

Every goal of Satan is to steal, kill and destroy, and your mind is his battlefield. The battles and attacks we face are of a spiritual nature. We cannot fight spiritual things with flesh or physical efforts, we need spiritual weapons.

"For though we walk in the flesh, we do not war according to the flesh. For the weapons of our warfare

are not carnal but mighty in God for pulling down strongholds, casting down arguments and every high thing that exalts itself against the knowledge of God, bringing every thought into captivity to the obedience of Christ, and being ready to punish all disobedience when your obedience is fulfilled." –2 Corinthians 10:3-6 (ESV)

Revelation of God's truth makes us free, so Satan attempts to set up strongholds, made up of unhealthy beliefs in our mind to block God's truth. Satan wants us to build ungodly strongholds, and God wants us to build godly strongholds. This doesn't mean a person is demon possessed. It means that Satan has a strong influence or grip on a person's belief system. Many people have ungodly strongholds (ungodly beliefs), which is why the Word of God tells us we must renew our mind (Romans 12:2). Paul says we must "*take every thought captive and make it obedient to Christ"* (Romans 12:21).

When ungodly strongholds (ungodly beliefs) are present, the devil has found a wound in that person that has not been healed. It is usually kept festering by bitterness and unforgiveness. He then uses those strongholds to keep people bound up in his lies, and wreck people's spiritual life, and contaminate the life of their family members.

Our Powerful Armor

In Ephesians Chapter 6, Paul talks about the whole Armor of God. He warns us that we are in a war, and that we must know how to defend ourselves. Understand that this spiritual war is for the eternal lives of the people around us, including our children. He shares with us the weapons of spiritual warfare that God has provided for us, which is the Armor of God, and how to use them.

Paul uses the Roman soldier's uniform to describe the tools that God has given us to fight the war we have been enlisted in. He says:

"[10] Finally, my brethren, be strong in the Lord and in the power of His might. [11] Put on the whole armor of God, that you may be able to stand against the wiles of the devil. [12] For we do not wrestle against flesh and blood, but against principalities, against powers, against the rulers of the darkness of this age, against spiritual hosts of wickedness in the heavenly places. [13] Therefore take up the whole armor of God, that you may be able to withstand in the evil day, and having done all, to stand.

¹⁴ Stand therefore, having girded your waist with truth, having put on the breastplate of righteousness, ¹⁵ and having shod your feet with the preparation of the gospel of peace; ¹⁶ above all, taking the shield of faith with which, you will be able to quench all the fiery darts of the wicked one. ¹⁷ And take the helmet of salvation, and the sword of the Spirit, which is the word of God; ¹⁸ praying always with all prayer and supplication in the Spirit, being watchful to this end with all perseverance and supplication for all the saints,"

The Armor of God is not something you put on every day like clothing. Neither is it something you put on just before a battle. The pieces of the Armor of God are convictions and beliefs that are to be lived as a regular way of life. Each piece is to be displayed in our daily life. Putting on the full armor of God means to apply all the Word of God to all your life.

A soldier's armor is defensive and offensive. The belt of truth, the breastplate of righteousness, feet fitted with the gospel of peace, the shield of faith and the helmet of salvation are defensive pieces of our armor. These pieces secure us, and help us block the attacks of the enemy. The sword of the spirit, which is the Word of God, is our only offensive weapon. This is what we are to fight and defeat the enemy with.

Our first piece of defense is the Belt of Truth. The belt of truth holds the other pieces of armor together. The devil will make accusations and lie to you about God and yourself. Without the belt of truth, we are vulnerable on the battlefield.

If you try to fight the enemy without the belt of truth, you will lose your pants and be shamefully exposed and destroyed. The sons of Sceva discovered this when they tried to take on the spiritual forces of evil without the truth (Acts 19:14-16). Many people are dropping their pants in battle because they don't have the belt of truth to keep them on.

The second piece of our defensive armor is the Breastplate of Righteousness. In the Roman soldier's uniform, the Breastplate is a piece of armor made from metal plates or thick leather that protects the vital organs from the neck to the waist. It particularly guards the heart. Just as he tries to sabotage the truth with his lies, Satan tries to pierce our hearts with flaming arrows of accusations. This is why we are told, *"Guard your heart more than anything else, because the source of your life flows from it"* (Proverbs 4:23).

There is only one thing that protects our heart against the devil's accusations, and that is righteousness. You can't be righteous by your own merits. Self-righteousness is not righteousness. The righteousness Paul is speaking of belongs to Christ. There is no righteousness outside of Christ.

2nd Corinthians 5:21 tells us that Jesus was made sin for us so that we might be made the righteousness of God in him. Wearing the breastplate of righteousness means to claim for yourself the righteousness before God that only comes from Christ, and then grow in obedience to Christ with His help. We wear the breastplate of righteousness because it protects us from all the enemy's devices. With the breastplate of righteousness on we pursue righteousness and turn away from sin.

The next piece of armor is feet shod with the preparation of the gospel of peace. Our feet are the foundation on which we stand, Jesus is that foundation. The word "gospel" means "good news," referring to the sacrifice of Jesus on the cross, which results in bringing us peace. When we understand our position in Christ, then we know that everything that is under His feet is also under our feet. As Christians, we are called to share the good news of the gospel with others. Knowing and understanding the gospel of Christ allows us to do this successfully. You should never go into a battle shoeless.

And then there is the shield of faith. The soldier's shield is vitally important, as it provides a blanket of protection. It was worn strapped to the soldier's arm, so at any time, it could be held up to deflect attacks. Having faith in God and His promises acts as a shield to protect us from the doubt and the lies thrown at us from the world. The shield of faith protects us from the arrows of anxiety, fear, discouragement, depression, low self-esteem, and everything else that the enemy throws at us.

Next there is the helmet of salvation is a crucial piece of spiritual armor. Helmets protect the brain, basically our minds. Your head is somewhere that your personal adversary, your enemy, will attack often because if he can affect you in your mind, he can affect your life. So, the helmet of salvation is a must for all Believers.

Finally, we are told to take the sword of the

spirit, which is God's Word. This includes God's written Word and God's spoken Word. God's word is living, and we can use His Word to defeat the enemy. We can speak God's Word over our lives for protection and safety. The final and one of the most vital parts of the armor is prayer. God is the commander of His spiritual army, and He alone knows how to lead it to victory, so we must also keep a steady connection with Him.

The story of the city of Jericho in the sixth Chapter of Joshua is the perfect biblical example of a spiritual stronghold, of how it operates in our life, and how God wants us to deal with them. The Bible says the inhabitants of Jericho built a wall around the city to protect it from their enemies. No enemy had been able to penetrate the walls before, yet the Israelites had to tear down the wall before they could possess what God said belonged to them.

"⁴ Now the gates of Jericho were securely barred because of the Israelites. No one went out and no one came in. ² Then the Lord said to Joshua, "See, I have delivered Jericho into your hands, along with its king and its fighting men. ³ March around the city once with all the armed men. Do this for six days. ⁴ Have seven priests carry trumpets of rams' horns in front

of the ark. On the seventh day, march around the city seven times, with the priests blowing the trumpets. ⁵ When you hear them sound a long blast on the trumpets, have the whole army give a loud shout; then the wall of the city will collapse and the army will go up, everyone straight in." –Joshua 6:1-5 (NIV)

After God freed the Israelites from Egypt, He told them that He would bring them into their own Promised Land. It would be a place of blessing and safety, flowing with milk and honey. After 40 years in the wilderness, and the death of Moses, God chose Joshua to lead the people of Israel to the Promised Land. When the Israelites finally came to the entrance of Canaan, the land God promised them, Jericho, a fortified city, blocked its entrance.

Scripture says that when the Israelites came to the city, the inhabitants of Jericho were afraid of them. Undoubtedly, they had heard about what God did on behalf of His children. As a Believer of Jesus Christ, Satan fears the Christ in you. Him and his demons know who you are. He knows *"you are from God and have overcome them, for he who is in you is greater than he who is in the world"* (1 John 4:4).

God knows that Israel could not overcome Jericho within their own strength and power. Since God has given them the land, He must intervene if His people are to possess it. Israel must rely on the strength and arm of God. Does that sound like a situation in your life right now? You've tried everything within your power to bring unity within your family, only to end up bouncing off the wall of division built up by Satan. The strongholds have created problems in our life, but the problems are opportunities for us to grow in our relationship with the Lord. God promised Joshua that He would deliver Jericho into their hands, and God is giving the same promise to us. *The seed of the righteous shall be delivered.*

All of us have a Jericho or two standing in the way of our ability to possess our possessions in Christ, in this case, restoration of your family. Regardless of the nature of our Jericho, we must realize victory always comes through God's plan of deliverance—never ours. God told Joshua to have the priests march around the city of Jericho for seven days, then blow their trumpets. On the seventh day when the people heard the sound of the trumpet, they shouted with a great shout and the wall fell down flat. We read in Hebrews 11:30, "by faith the walls of Jericho fell down ..."

I don't know why God did it this way, but I do know that only God and faith in the truth of His word can destroy a stronghold. Ask God to show you any strongholds that you may be dealing with, then allow Him to help you deal with them according to His word, His grace, and His power.

God's Sovereign Will

I have heard many times that God will not go against a person's own free will. You may have heard that, too. Many Believers accept the thought that God never violates a person's own free will as truth, overriding what God has said in His Word. Truth is, when it comes to salvation and many other instances in our life, it is necessary for God to intervene and go against our will and desires.

Jeremiah 17:9 says the natural state of man's heart is deceitful and desperately wicked. Before being born again, we are carnally minded, not spiritually minded. The carnal mind is enmity against God. It is not subject to the Law of God, neither indeed can it be (Romans 8:6-7). So, unless God violates or goes against our free will, none of us would ever become born again.

2nd Corinthians 4:4 tells us, *"The god of this age (Satan) has blinded the minds of unbelievers, so that they cannot see the light of the gospel."* Before we were born again, we were dead in trespasses and sins (Ephesians 2:1-3). Although our bodies were alive, we were spiritually dead men and women walking around in the earth, confined in the sin nature that we inherited from Adam. We naturally lived and acted according to the prince of the power of the air, who is Satan. So, this cannot be considered free will!

Just as a prisoner is constrained by the walls and the locked door of his prison cell, we were constrained by our sin nature. Even though it is his will to be free, the prisoner is locked in until he is set free, so it is for mankind. Jesus came to set the captive free! (Luke 4:18)

Look at the following Scriptures which unmistakably point out God's sovereignty:

Exodus 4:11 – The Lord said to him, "Who has made man's mouth? Or who makes him mute or deaf, or seeing or blind? Is it not I, the Lord?"

Psalm 135:6 – Whatever the Lord pleases, He does, in heaven and in earth, in the seas and in all deeps.

Proverbs 21:1 – The king's heart is like channels of water in the hand of the Lord; He turns it wherever He wishes.

Proverbs 16:1 – The plans of the heart belong to man, but the answer of the tongue is from the Lord.

Proverbs 16:9 – *The mind of man plans his way, but the Lord directs his steps.*

Proverbs 16:33 – *The lot is cast into the lap, but its every decision is from the Lord.*

Proverbs 19:21 – *Many plans are in a man's heart, but the counsel of the Lord will stand.*

Job 42:2 – *I know that You can do all things, and that no purpose of Yours can be thwarted.*

Isaiah 46:9-10 – *For I am God, and there is no other; I am God, and there is no one like Me, declaring the end from the beginning, and from ancient times things which have not been done, saying, 'My purpose will be established, and I will accomplish all My good pleasure.'*

Isaiah 64:8 – *But now, O Lord, You are our Father, we are the clay, and You, our potter; and all of us are the work of Your hand.*

Jeremiah 1:4 – *Now the word of the Lord came to me saying, 'Before I formed you in the womb I knew you, and before you were born I consecrated you; I have appointed you a prophet to the nations.'*

Lamentations 3:37-38 – *Who is there who speaks, and it comes to pass, unless the Lord has commanded it?*

So, there is no denying God's sovereignty. As I

think more about man's free will vs. God's sovereignty, I think about how when Jonah ran away from his assignment to go to Nineveh, God did not respect his free will to reject his assignment. No, God orchestrated circumstances, and Jonah ultimately chose to go where God wanted him to go. What about Paul? Even though he thought he was doing God's will by persecuting Christians, the Lord Jesus Christ interrupted his plans, and once Paul learned the truth, he changed his will to God's will.

So, does God go against our will? I don't really think it matters all that much because God has declared the end from the beginning. His purpose will stand, and He will accomplish all His good pleasure (Isaiah 46:10). We do have the freedom to choose to do as we please, however, our will is subordinate to God's will. God has decreed certain things over our lives according to His plan and purpose. If our choice conflicts with the will, plan, and purpose of God, His plan will always prevail. He can, and often does use His sovereign power to influence the outcome of situations so that His will is done.

God makes it clear that He does not want any person to perish. Neither does He take pleasure in the death of the wicked. He wants everyone to embrace the life He offers through His Son. So, when we pray for our children to repent and turn to the Lord, we are praying according to His will, and we are, in essence praying that God will intervene in their rebellion. Do you agree?

Trust The Process

A process is a series of actions or steps taken in order to achieve a particular end. God will do what needs to be done to bring about the deliverance of your family, but you've got to trust Him through the process. A friend and I were having a discussion, and I said that God will go through extremes to deliver us out of bondage. I used the example of God splitting the Red Sea to deliver the nation of Israel.

The Bible tells us that the Israelites left Egypt at nighttime after Passover. God told Israel that He would smite Egypt's firstborn at "midnight" (Exodus 12:29). Right after the firstborn were killed Pharaoh summoned Moses and Aaron and asked them to take God's children and leave Egypt (verse 31).

Scripture says,

"It was a night of watching by the Lord, to bring them out of the land of Egypt; so this same night is a

night of watching kept to the Lord by all the people of Israel throughout their generations." – Exodus 12:42

"[51] And on that very day the Lord brought the people of Israel out of the land of Egypt by their hosts. – Exodus 12:51

So, as we read on in Exodus Chapter 14,

"[19] Then the angel of God who was going before the host of Israel moved and went behind them, and the pillar of cloud moved from before them and stood behind them, [20] coming between the host of Egypt and the host of Israel. And there was the cloud and the darkness. And it lit up the night without one coming near the other all night.

[21] Then Moses stretched out his hand over the sea, and the Lord drove the sea back by a strong east wind all night and made the sea dry land, and the waters were divided. [22] And the people of Israel went into the midst of the sea on dry ground, the waters being a wall to them on their right hand and on their left. [23] The Egyptians pursued and went in after them into the midst of the sea, all Pharaoh's horses, his chariots, and his horsemen." – Exodus 14:19-23 ESV

Scripture says God drove back the waters all

that night.

> *"²⁴ And in the morning watch the Lord in the pillar of fire and of cloud looked down on the Egyptian forces and threw the Egyptian forces into a panic, ²⁵ clogging their chariot wheels so that they drove heavily. And the Egyptians said, "Let us flee from before Israel, for the Lord fights for them against the Egyptians."*
>
> *²⁶ Then the Lord said to Moses, "Stretch out your hand over the sea, that the water may come back upon the Egyptians, upon their chariots, and upon their horsemen." ²⁷ So Moses stretched out his hand over the sea, and the sea returned to its normal course when the morning appeared. And as the Egyptians fled into it, the Lord threw the Egyptians into the midst of the sea.*
>
> *²⁸ The waters returned and covered the chariots and the horsemen; of all the host of Pharaoh that had followed them into the sea, not one of them remained. ²⁹ But the people of Israel walked on dry ground through the sea, the waters being a wall to them on their right hand and on their left." – Exodus 14:24-29 ESV*

Oh, my!!! Are you shouting yet? Every time I

think about this miracle that God performed, I am reminded of just how powerful the God we serve is. And the lengths that He will go through to deliver His children. You and your seed are His children. Our mighty and miraculous God delivered His children in one night. Isn't He amazing? He put a pep in the step of millions of people as they walked across a sea on dry land, but Pharoah's chariots got stuck in the mud and drowned. If He delivered an entire nation, He can certainly deliver your seed.

I know God brought this passage to my heart to encourage me in the battle, and it did. Scripture says that the enemy will always come to attack your faith, trying to make you doubt God's Word (Mark 4:15). Immediately after I declared this powerful statement that I truly believe, a thought came to my mind about my sons, and I began to feel weak and despondent. Before I knew it, I was voicing those thoughts. My friend said to me, "Angeline you are either going to trust God concerning the situation with your sons, or you're going to worry. Which shall you do?" Those words really humbled me, and woke me up out of the slumber of grief I was headed into. Understand that none of us are above being ministered to and getting weak in the battle, but if you pay attention, God will always have a way of escape prepared for you.

This is why it is important to have godly spouses, godly friends, and godly leaders in your life who will pray for you, speak the Word of God over you, and to you. We need people in our life who are not afraid to speak truth to us and to be used by God. So, mom, dad, I know it hurts, really bad, but I remind you that God is still God. He is a God of unity, relationship, and love. He is a God who keeps His promises. He rescued and sustained His people, and He did it in a way only He can do.

Like most of us, Moses wanted quick success. I imagine he thought because God had commissioned him to free Israel that he could walk up to Pharaoh, and he would immediately let Israel go. But that is not what happened, and Moses didn't understand why. He asked God, "Why did you send me? I went before Pharaoh in Your name, but he just laughed at me and placed a heavier burden on the people" (Exodus 5:22-23 paraphrased).

Nine times God commanded Pharaoh to *"Let my people go that they may serve me"* (Exodus 5:1–10:4). After each command, Pharaoh's pride prevented him from making the wise choice to follow

God's commands. Have you ever talked to your children and tried to reason with them until you were blue in the face? Have you ever prayed about a situation, and the more you pray, the worst things seemed to get? Satan has no new strategies. That same spirit of pride that controlled Pharoah is prevalent in society today, and in your family. But it has no power against a blood bought Believer who knows who they are in Christ... you declare out of your mouth, "*Devil, let my child go that they may serve the Lord. For it is written the seed of the righteous shall be delivered!*" Then stand on that declaration and see the salvation of the Lord. Every time the enemy tries to make you doubt, shout it out.

Beauty for Ashes

"To appoint unto them that mourn in Zion, to give unto them beauty for ashes, the oil of joy for mourning, the garment of praise for the spirit of heaviness, that they might be called trees of righteousness, the planting of the Lord, that he might be glorified." – Isaiah 61:3

David's experience at Ziklag serves as an inspiration to all who would arise out of seeming defeat. Throughout this book, it has been my goal to impress upon you that God cares about what you're going through, and He wants you whole, and complete: spirit, soul, and body (1st Thessalonians 5:23). Sorrow can leave us feeling defeated. Maybe the estrangement in your family has caused you to wonder does God really love you. Does God love your child?

When we focus on our problems, all of us can find ourselves wondering about God's love. Isaiah 61:3 is a beautiful reminder that God can take the worst of circumstances and turn it into something great. It gives us hope that we will come out on the other side of sorrow with shouts of praise for our Lord.

Ashes are the remains, or ruins of something destroyed by flames. They are the residue of the the grief, agony, and heartache in our life. There have been many times in my life that the heat from painful circumstances seemed so hot that it felt like I was engulfed in a fiery furnace. But because of God's amazing love and faithfulness, I learned to trust that God would somehow restore me from the damage done.

I'm often reminded of Shadrach, Meshach, and Abednego, the three Hebrew men who were thrown in a fiery furnace, but no harm came to them (Daniel 3:8-25). When King Nebuchadnezzar looked into the furnace, he couldn't believe what he saw! He said, "I see four men unbound, walking in the midst of the fire, and they are not hurt; and the appearance of the fourth is like a son of the gods."

God does not intend for us to stay stuck in our pain and sorrow. If we can accept the grief of estrangement, then we can overcome it. If we carry our sorrow and lay it at the foot of the cross and leave it there, an exchange takes place. The circumstances may remain the same, but the glass we look through will change. We begin to look through the glass of faith rather than sorrow. We may not instantly feel happy, but our heart will feel lighter when we trust God to work the situation out.

I want you to know and believe that you are the apple of God's eye. The apple of one's eye is its center. This means you are cherished by God. He held the rebellious and stiff-necked nation of Israel as the apple of His eye (Zechariah 2:8-10). Even though they were in the wilderness, they were the apple of His eye. Even in the midst of what is happening in your family right now, you and your children are the apple of God's eye. You are what God focuses on. He loves and cherishes you, not because you've impressed Him so much, or because you are such a perfect child, but simply because you are His child. You are everything to Him.

In Malachi 1:2, God told Israel, *"I have always loved you."* He's saying to you, *"I have always loved you. Through all your mistakes, I have loved you. Through all your sins, I have loved you. Through all your rebellion, I have loved you. I have never stopped loving you, and I never will."* God is a restorer and a redeemer. Because God loves you so much, He takes the hurtful things that have happened in your life and transforms them into something beautiful. He is really good at too. Then He uses us to help others overcome their damaged lives. But it starts with us surrendering the pain and sorrow to Him, which allows Him to redeem and repair us.

Sometimes it can be difficult to surrender in the midst of pain and sorrow. God's strength is made perfect in our weakness. Joy and peace are found in knowing that God loves us (John 3:16). If we focus on God's love for us, rather than our love for God, we will experience the peace and joy that belongs to us because of Christ, who lives in us. Focusing on how much God loves us reminds us that His love isn't based on what we do or say, but on the fact that God is an unconditional, loving God.

Unlike people, we cannot make God stop loving us. God loves us too much to leave us. We can complain and get angry at Him, but it will not stop Him from loving us. Believe me, once we focus on how much He loves us, we can easily lay our troubles at the foot of the Cross. Because He loves us, He is watching over His written and spoken word to us to perform it.

God has never failed, and He never will, and His love is not going to fail in our life either. Somehow, someway, God's love for us is going to show up. He will restore, repair, and give us beauty for ashes. God cannot give you beauty for your ashes if you continue to hold onto them. Let them go.

Let Go and Let God

One thought that troubled me regarding the estrangement between me and my sons, was should I stop reaching out? I felt that if I stopped, I would be abandoning them. You may be having the same or similar thoughts. The decision to continue or to stop reaching out to your estranged child is a personal one. I'm not a licensed therapist, so I can only share my opinion and my experience on the matter.

> *God's love for us isn't based on what we do or say, but on the fact that God is an unconditional, loving God.*

For a while I felt that I needed to continue reaching out to my sons to let them know I love them, and wanted them in my life. Then I would wait to hear back from them, thinking this time, things would be different. If they responded, it would start a barrage of horrible responses, and my heart would be broken again. Each time they didn't respond, I experienced more grief. As I said earlier, the grief of adult child parent estrangement is similar to that of the death of a child. Having experienced both, sometimes the grief feels the same.

Grief is very stressful on the body. It releases stress hormones in your body which can lead to new health issues or intensify existing conditions. One time, after reaching out to my sons with no response, it bothered me so much that I started experiencing chest pain and I ended up in the emergency room.

Since the emergency room incident, and having had a massive heart attack in the past, which I believe resulted from grief, I decided that continuing to reach out to my sons was not healthy for me, so I prayed and released the situation to God. God saw the struggle I was having with the decision, and He gave me Acts 26:17-18 to stand on. In the passage, He was talking to Paul, but God knew I needed deliverance as well, and this is what He said:

"[17] And I will rescue you from both your own people and the Gentiles. Yes, I am sending you to the Gentiles [18] to open their eyes, so they may turn from darkness to light and from the power of Satan to God. Then they will receive forgiveness for their sins and be given a place among God's people, who are set apart by faith in me.'"

I can't explain it, but that passage came alive in me, especially the words, *"I will rescue you from both."* Up until that point it was like I was stuck in the ugliness of the situation, but when I meditated and prayed on the passage, I received an unexplainable peace, and hope that God will deliver my family. When I say I prayed the passage I mean that I prayed something like this:

"Father God, thank You for rescuing me and my sons. For turning them from darkness to light and from the power of Satan to God. Thank You for making us ready to go forth and open the eyes of others, so they may also turn from darkness to light and from the power of Satan to God, and receive forgiveness for their sins, and be given a place among God's people, who are set apart by faith in Jesus Christ."

Listen, it's okay to feel the pain of not having your children or grandchildren in your life. I actually think it is unavoidable. It is normal to wish things were different, or even to feel a sense of guilt in getting on with your life. Come on now, we are talking about our child(ren) and grandchildren. However, like I said earlier, we cannot let the abandonment and grief debilitate us.

Ecclesiastes 3:1-8 says,

"¹ To every thing there is a season, and a time to every purpose under the heaven: ² A time to be born, and a time to die; a time to plant, and a time to pluck up that which is planted; ³ A time to kill, and a time to heal; a time to break down, and a time to build up; ⁴ A time to weep, and a time to laugh; a time to mourn, and a time to dance; ⁵ A time to cast away

stones, and a time to gather stones together; a time to embrace, and a time to refrain from embracing; ^{6} *A time to get, and a time to lose; a time to keep, and a time to cast away;* ^{7} *A time to rend, and a time to sew; a time to keep silence, and a time to speak;* ^{8} *A time to love, and a time to hate; a time of war, and a time of peace.*

"Give all your worries and cares to God, for He cares about you."

The Scripture says there is a season of weeping, and a season of mourning, but they are just that, seasons. Seasons pass and seasons change. We are not supposed to build a summer home and live there. Through the power of God, I was pulled out of what was trying to hold me captive, and I stood up in God's power, so I could keep going forward. This doesn't mean that I have given up hope that my family will be restored. I continue to you declare, "*Devil, let my sons go that they may serve the Lord. For it is written the seed of the righteous shall be delivered!*"

In 1st Peter 5:7 (NLT) Peter encourages us to *"Give all your worries and cares to God, for He cares about you."* Like most of us, Peter had to learn to cast his cares on the Lord through trial and error. He put his foot in his mouth often, and he had his own way of doing things. It took Peter some time to grow to the point that he could trust that Jesus knew best and had his best interest in mind. Eventually, he learned to step down into the greatness that Jesus called him to, when He said, follow me and I will make you fishers of men (Matthew 4:18-19).

Have you ever heard the phrase let go and let God? Years ago, when problems and situations arose, I would say "Father, I'm letting this go. I put it all in Your hands." Then I would worry and take on the problem trying to work things out myself. Only to end up frustrated with a bigger mess than I started with. Then I had to ask God to forgive me for not trusting Him, and release the problem to Him again, so He could clean up the mess I made. I thank God that He is faithful and merciful.

When Jesus was about to undergo the most difficult punishments, any human can endure, to help him do this, He yielded Himself to the will of the Father. He let go of His desire, and His will, and He prayed, *"Father, if thou be willing, remove this cup from me: nevertheless, not my will, but thine, be done."* Letting go and letting God frees you to focus on moving forward in peace as you wait for Him to work in your situation. Letting go and letting God have His way in our life is the best thing we can do in any situation. When my desire is contrary to God's Word, I have learned to turn to Him in prayer for strength. Prayer was a way of life for Jesus, and it should be for us as well.

Letting go and letting God does not mean you stop living, give up, become complacent, and do nothing until your situation changes. No, you don't take on the attitude of God is sovereign and in control, and there is nothing I can do, so why even try. Letting go and letting God means we don't try to control our situations or meet our needs in our own strength, but we surrender to God and live from a surrendered position. God may not give you every detail of what you should do ahead of time. You've got to trust Him through the process.

I've also learned to trust that if God brings me to it, He will bring me through it. If He allows it, He has a plan. Sometimes I miss the mark on that one, but I repent and keep going. God's mercies are new every morning. What happened yesterday is gone. Dragging around the past only takes up space for God's goodness, grace, and favor for today.

In Matthew 14:22-33, Jesus told the disciples to get in the boat and go ahead of him to the other side of the sea, while he dismissed the crowd. He dismissed the crowd and went off to pray. By the time He finished, it was evening, and the boat was in the middle of the sea, being tossed by waves and wind. Jesus comes walking on the water towards the boat.

Seeing Him approaching, and not sure of who it was, Peter and the disciples became afraid. Jesus saw their fear and spoke to them, saying, *"Be of good cheer! It is I; do not be afraid."* Peter said to Him, *"Lord, if it is You, command me to come to You on the water."* Jesus said, *"Come."*

Letting go and letting God is impossible to do without God empowering you to do it. Peter didn't know how he would walk on the water to Jesus, but he trusted that Jesus would empower him to do it. He got out of the boat, and walked on the water to go to Jesus. But when he saw the wind raging, he became afraid. When he let fear take over, He began to sink. Then he cried out, *"Lord, save me!"* Immediately Jesus stretched out His hand and caught him, and said to him, *"O you of little faith, why did you doubt?"* When they got into the boat, the wind ceased.

When it comes to continuing to reach out to

your estranged child, I don't believe there is a right or wrong thing to do. Whether you let go or whether you keep reaching out and getting no response, you will experience pain. Keep the door open, but lower your expectations. Don't pin all your hopes on them responding. God does not want you to continue to live with the guilt, shame, and sorrow this situation has brought. He wants you to stop crying and celebrate the life you have. Keeping your eyes on the One who can calm the stormy sea is the key to getting through this difficult journey.

Letting go and letting God is impossible to do without God empowering you to do it.

So, examine whether it's healthy and wise for you to continue to reach out, take a break, or to stop entirely. Talk to God about it and do what He leads you to do. Seek the Word of God and apply it to the situation. One Scripture to consider is Matthew 6:33 which says, *"But seek ye first the kingdom of God, and his righteousness; and all these things shall be added unto you."* That is a powerful promise. Put God first and get and He will take care of everything else. Give Him time to work on your child, and then when God releases you to reach out again, do so with His blessing.

Remove The Grave Clothes

In John Chapter 11 we find the story of Lazarus, one of Jesus' friends who got sick. When this happened, Jesus was in another town preaching the Good News and healing people (John 11:25-44). Lazarus' two sisters, Mary, and Martha sent word to Jesus that his friend was very sick, to come pray for him, but Jesus didn't arrive in time, and Lazarus died. When Jesus finally got to Bethany, Lazarus had been dead for four days.

When Martha heard that Jesus was coming, she went to Him and said, "Lord, if You had been here, my brother would not have died. But even now I know that whatever You ask of God, God will give You." Jesus said to her, "Your brother will rise again."

"I know that he will rise again in the resurrection at the last day," Martha replied. Then Jesus said, "I am the resurrection and the life. He who believes in Me, though he may die, he shall live. And whoever lives and believes in Me shall never die. Do you believe this?" "Yes, Lord, I believe You are the

Christ, the Son of God, who is to come into the world," she said.

In that day, when a person died, the family would often wrap them in burial clothes, like a mummy, and put them in a tomb and seal it with a large stone. When Mary got there and saw Jesus she fell at His feet, saying to Him, "Lord, if You had been here, my brother would not have died."

Although Jesus knew He was about to perform a miracle, He was so moved by Lazarus' death and the sadness of his family that He cried and asked, "Where have you laid him?" Some of the people mocked, saying, "Could not this Man, who opened the eyes of the blind, also have kept this man from dying?" This lets us know that there will always be someone around to mock your faith. Pay them no mind!

When they got to the tomb, Jesus said, "Take away the stone." Martha replied, "But Lord, he has been dead four days. By this time, he stinks." Jesus said, "Did I not tell you that if you believe, you will see the glory of God?" They took away the stone, and Jesus lifted up His eyes and said, "Father, I thank You that You have heard Me. And I know that You always hear Me, but I said this for the benefit of the people standing here, that they may believe that You sent me."

Jesus then spoke to Lazarus, saying, "Lazarus, come forth." Lazarus woke up and walked out of the tomb. Although Lazarus had received an extraordinary miracle, although Lazarus was already delivered by the Word and power of God, although he had been resurrected to a new life, he was still wrapped in grave clothes. His hands and feet were bound, and his face wrapped with a cloth. Jesus said to them, "Take off the grave clothes, loose him, and let him go."

Think about what the people around must have thought, having never seen a person walk out of a tomb before, let alone someone who had been dead four days and stinking. I can only imagine the courage and faith it took to walk up there, and carefully remove the layers of wrappings.

Martha thought her brother Lazarus was too far gone for anything to be done. She was mourning his death as if Jesus, the miracle worker, could not change the situation. Things may be bad. Your child may be bound by past hurt, addictions, unbelief, fear, anger, and more, and Satan wants you to mourn their spiritual death, and what could have been. Cast that liar aside and trust God! You have Jesus, the Miracle Worker in you to remove their grave clothes.

Praying for and declaring God's Word over our children is one of God's greatest gifts as a parent, even if they are grown and gone. Speak faith into them, even if from a distance. Love and care for them as they allow you. As a parent of adult children, it's hard to watch the battle from the sidelines, but your most powerful weapon is prayer. Declare God's Word over them. Declare their freedom. Be a grave clothes remover and intercede for your child. *(see Scriptures To Pray Over Your Children)*

Praying With Holy Anger

I woke up early one morning with holy anger inside. Holy anger is sometimes called righteous anger. It is the type of anger that David experienced when he said of Goliath, *"who is this uncircumcised Philistine that dares to defy the Army of the Living God?"* (1st Samuel 17:26) It is the type of anger Jesus felt when He walked into the temple and saw that the Scribes and the Pharisees had turned the house of God into a flea market. He got so angry that He flipped the tables over and drove out all who were buying and selling there. He declared, *"It is written, 'My house shall be called a house of prayer,' but you have made it a 'den of thieves."* (Matthew 21:13).

Jesus also exhibited holy anger in Mark 3:1-5:

"¹ And He entered the synagogue again, and a man was there who had a withered hand. ² So they watched Him closely, whether He would heal him on the Sabbath, so that they might accuse Him. ³ And He said to the man who had the withered hand, "Step forward."⁴ Then He said to them, "Is it lawful on the Sabbath to do good or to do evil, to save life or to kill?" But they kept silent. ⁵ And when He had looked around at them with anger, being grieved by the hardness of their hearts, He said to the man, "Stretch out your hand." And he stretched it out, and his hand was restored as whole as the other."

Holy or righteous anger is an anger that is grieved by sin, death, and any other form of evil. Holy or righteous anger arises in Believers when we see an offense against God, His Word, or mistreatment, or malice of another, and a desire for things to be made right.

I was angry at the evil that has touched my sons

and other adult children and caused them to alienate their parents. They are hated and being deceived, and mistreated by Satan, and it is insulting to God and who He says they are. Let me be clear, we are not to hate people. We are to hate the evil that Satan has them bound in, and pray for the Lord to set them free from captivity. *The seed of the righteous shall be delivered.*

Satan has attempted to destroy your family by hardening the heart of your child(ren) against you, and he has tried to harden your heart against your child(ren). However, God has a hammer that will break the hardness of heart into pieces. God says in Jeremiah 23:29 that His Word is like fire and like a hammer that breaks the rock in pieces. When something is burned up, no one will ever be able to take its ashes and rebuild the object.

A hammer is used to break hard stones. Now, imagine using a hammer and breaking a rock into pieces. No one will ever be able to put those pieces back together again. When you declare the Word of God over your situation, family, and child(ren) it is like giving repeated blows to the situation and stubborn hearts and burns up everything that Satan has tried to build.

Here are some Scripture promises that you can use to break the hardness of estrangement into pieces. The next time you think of the situation between you and your child, let Holy anger arise and declare the Word of God over your seed. Continue to declare God's Word giving repeated blows to the stubbornness until their heart becomes ready to be re-shaped according to the will of the Heavenly Father.

Jeremiah 29:11 – *For I know the thoughts that I think toward you, says the LORD, thoughts of peace and not of evil, to give you a future and a hope.*

I declare that God has a plan for my children that will bring only joy and hope. May His plan be done on earth as it is done in Heaven. My children will find, follow, and flow in the perfect will of God. From this moment forward only God's best will touch my children. God's divine plan will be accomplished for my child(ren).

Jeremiah 31:16 – *"This is what the LORD says: "Restrain your voice from weeping and your eyes from tears, for your work will be rewarded," declares the LORD. "They will return from the land of the* *enemy."*

I declare that my voice will restrain from weeping and my eyes from tears, for the Lord has declared that my work will be rewarded, and that my child(ren) will return from the land of the enemy."

Isaiah 10:27 *– "It shall come to pass in that day that his burden will be taken away from your shoulder, and his yoke from your neck, and the yoke will be destroyed because of the anointing oil."*

I declare that God's presence is always upon my child(ren). They shall walk in and under the anointing of God. The power of God is continually flowing in and through my child(ren)'s lives.

Isaiah 59:21 *– "This is my promise to them," says the LORD. "My Spirit, who is on you, and my words that I put in your mouth will not leave you. They will be with your children and your grandchildren permanently," says the LORD.*

I declare that the Word of God will be with my child(ren) and my grandchildren permanently.

Isaiah 44:3 *– "For I will give you abundant water*

for your thirst and for your parched fields. And I will pour out my Spirit and my blessings on your children."

I declare that God's blessings are upon me and my family. His provision finds us like streams and rivers. God's Spirit covers my children, and His blessings are upon us.

Isaiah 49:25 *– "But the Lord says, "Even the captives of the most mighty and most terrible shall all be freed; for I will fight those who fight you, and I will save your children.*

I declare that my child(ren) and my grandchildren shall all be freed; for the Lord God will fight those who fight us, and He will save my child(ren) and my grandchildren.

Psalm 35:27 *– "...let them say continually, "Let the LORD be magnified, Who has pleasure in the prosperity of His servant."*

God delights to prosper His servants. I declare that my child(ren) and my grandchildren will serve God all the days of their lives and honor His Word. They shall be blessed all the days of their lives. No harm will touch my children.

Only blessings will come upon my child(ren) and my grandchildren. Blessings are being sent to me and my children every day by the love of God.

Luke 2:52 – *"And Jesus increased in wisdom and stature, and in favor with God and men."*

I declare that my child(ren) are clothed with favor from upon high, and they are growing in wisdom and favor with God and man.

Colossians 2:2 – *"That their hearts may be encouraged, being knit together in love, and attaining to all riches of the full assurance of understanding, to the knowledge of the mystery of God, both of the Father and of Christ,*

I declare that my child(ren) are being knit by the Spirit of God to me, their siblings, godly friends and relationships. This family is restored.

Valley Of Dry Bones

I cannot express enough how powerful speaking God's Word over your life and circumstances is. Can I tell you a story about Ezekiel and the Valley of Dry Bones, which is found in Ezekiel 37:1-10? Although it happened thousands of years ago, this is a prophetic word to every Believer who is crying out to God to resurrect family relationships, finances, health, or whatever seems dead in their life.

The bones in the valley represent the nation of Israel, who for centuries had been living in sin and rebellion, confident in their own strength, as if they didn't need God. God continually sent warnings, prophetic messages, and even invasions, to get their attention and remind them of their identity and His holy nature.

Finally, because of their continued rebellion, God removed them from their promised land and sent them into captivity in Babylon. I want to point out that God didn't exile the Israelites just to punish them for punishment's sake. He wanted to bring His people to a state of repentance and humility.

When God spoke to Ezekiel in Chapter 37, the Israelites had been in Babylon for ten years and had lost hope and they needed a miracle and began to cry out to God. Again, God heard their cry and speaks a prophetic word to His prophet.

Ezekiel 37:1-3: "[1] The hand of the Lord was upon me, and he brought me out in the Spirit of the Lord and set me down in the middle of the valley; it was full of bones. [2] And he led me around among them, and behold, there were very many on the surface of the valley, and behold, they were very dry. [3] And he said to me, "Son of man, can these bones live?" And I answered, "O Lord God, you know."[4] Then he said to me, "Prophesy over these bones, and say to them, O dry bones, hear the word of the Lord.

The bones Ezekiel sees in the valley were not the skeleton of one person in one place. They were bones of several people that had been broken and scattered all over the valley. Not one bone was in its correct position to make a skeleton. In other words, Israel's hope as a nation had completely dried up.

God asked, "*Son of man, can these bones live?*"

Ezekiel answered, *"O Lord God, you know."*

Prophesy means to reveal by divine inspiration; to reveal the will or message of God. Prophesying is speaking what God says, whether in His Word or through a Rhema word through a person or into a situation. Ezekiel prophesied the Word of God over the dead, dry bones, and literally called them back to life. He commanded them to hear the word of the Lord. The Word of the Lord carries the life, and authority of the Lord.

You may be thinking, but God spoke directly to Ezekiel. And to that, I say God is speaking directly to you too through His Word. God says that He will watch over His Word to perform it. When we decree the Word of God, we are giving voice to His Word.

'Thus says the Lord God to these bones: Behold, I will cause breath to enter you, and you shall live. ⁶ And I will lay sinews upon you, and will cause flesh to come upon you, and cover you with skin, and put breath in you, and you shall live, and you shall know that I am the Lord."

Each person's dried bones were gathered from

wherever they were in the valley and put back together, and then that person's flesh and blood was placed back on them. What an amazing miracle! This is mind-blowing. Only God is able to do this. Even more than that, notice Ezekiel's obedience and faith. This was seemingly impossible, yet Ezekiel knew God's word had supernatural power and prophesied what God spoke. He knew that *"The things which are impossible with men are possible with God"* (Luke 18:27). He was confident that if God said it, and he spoke what God said, it would supernaturally happen.

> *"So I prophesied as I was commanded. And as I prophesied, there was a sound, and behold, a rattling, and the bones came together, bone to its bone. And I looked, and behold, there were sinews on them, and flesh had come upon them, and skin had covered them. But there was no breath in them."*

Like the bones in valley, God wants to revive the "dead" things in our life. He wants to pull your family back together. Can God really cause the love to be restored between you and your children? Can anything great come from a past of failure? Yes! Absolutely, yes! What we may see as a hopeless, dry, and dead situation, God sees as an opportunity to show His power in our lives, especially to those around us. Obedience helps revival to come. Ezekiel prophesied into a bleak situation as he was commanded.

> *"Then he said to me, "Prophesy to the breath; prophesy, son of man, and say to the breath, Thus says the Lord God: Come from the four winds, O breath, and breathe on these slain, that they may live." So I prophesied as he commanded me, and the breath came into them, and they lived and stood on their feet, an exceedingly great army." – Ezekiel 37:9-10*

Now, Ezekiel is told to call upon the breath, which symbolizes the Holy Spirit. As the word of God was proclaimed over them, the wind of the Holy Spirit blew on the bones, and they received God's promise of life. The same Power that put the bones back together in the valley can fix what is broken in your life, including your family. Our responsibility is to pray, prophesy and proclaim God's power and life to those dead places in our life, our family and relationships, in our churches, and in the hearts of those who don't know their Jesus as LORD yet.

Once God breathed life into the skeletons, they became an exceedingly great army, who acted under the orders of the one who gave them life. Notice that the reviving of the dry bones happened in stages:

- Stirring of the bones.
- Assembly of the bones.
- Sinews and flesh upon the bones.
- Skin upon the tissues covering the bones.
- God breathing upon the assembled bones.

This lets us know that reviving your family and the dead things in your life will be a process. Let me remind you that the same Spirit (Breath) of Him who raised Jesus from the dead dwells in you (Romans 8:11). When you speak the Word of God, your words will go out and accomplish what God wants to them to do. Use God's Word to declare healing in your family. Use God's Word to speak salvation to your children. Do you hear what I hear?" If so, prophesy to your life today and let the wind of the Spirit flow into you! Listen, the devil has been prophesying to you. It's time you prophesy to him!

Pray The Word of God Over Your Adult Children

When I pray God's Word, I personalize specific Scriptures according to the need. I've added examples throughout this book and included Scriptures that I pray and confess. You can find use these scriptures to pray according to your need, or ask God for a Word to stand on according to your situation. Then, pray it each day for a week, a month, or however long it takes to get it settled in your spirit, or until you receive a breakthrough. I pray some scripture daily.

Here are a few promises of God that we can pray over our children. 2nd Corinthians 1:20 says, *"ALL the promises of God are YES in Christ, and through Him the Amen is spoken by us to the glory of God."* The "Amen" is a word of declaration that confirms we believe. Also remember, as you pray, I am praying with you. God may show you more. Let us pray... *(insert your child's name in the blank).*

Acts 16:31: ... *"Believe on the Lord Jesus Christ, and you will be saved, you and your household."*

Heavenly Father I ask You to help _____

believe in the Lord Jesus, and be saved. Them and their household.

Galatians 5:22-23: *"But the fruit of the Spirit is love, joy, peace, longsuffering, kindness, goodness, faithfulness, gentleness, self-control. Against such there is no law."*

Heavenly Father I ask You to fill my _____with Your Holy Spirit and help them to understand and walk in the fruit of the Spirit, which is love, joy, peace, patience, kindness, goodness, faithfulness, gentleness, and self-control.

Ephesians 1:17-19: *"that the God of our Lord Jesus Christ, the Father of glory, may give to you the spirit of wisdom and revelation in the knowledge of Him, the eyes of your understanding being enlightened; that you may know what is the hope of His calling, what are the riches of the glory of His inheritance in the saints, and what is the exceeding greatness of His power toward us who believe, according to the working of His mighty power."*

Father God, I ask You to give _____ the spirit

of wisdom and revelation in the knowledge of Him. Open _____'s eyes of understanding so that they may know the hope to which You have called them, the riches of Jesus' glorious inheritance in the saints, and what the exceeding greatness of His power is to those who believe, according to the working of His mighty power.

Colossians 1:9-12: *"For this reason we also, since the day we heard it, do not cease to pray for you, and to ask that you may be filled with the knowledge of His will in all wisdom and spiritual understanding; that you may walk worthy of the Lord, fully pleasing Him, being fruitful in every good work and increasing in the knowledge of God; strengthened with all might, according to His glorious power, for all patience and longsuffering with joy; giving thanks to the Father who has qualified us to be partakers of the inheritance of the saints in the light."*

Father God, I ask You to fill _____ with the knowledge of the Your will in all spiritual wisdom and understanding, that _____ may walk in a manner worthy of the Lord, pleasing to Him: bearing fruit in every good work and increasing in the knowledge of God. Father I ask You to strengthen _____ with all power, according to His glorious might, for all endurance and patience with joy; giving thanks to You Father, who qualifies them to share in the inheritance of the saints in light.

Proverbs 3:5-6: *"Trust in the Lord with all your heart, and lean not on your own understanding; In all your ways acknowledge Him, and He shall direct your paths."*

Heavenly Father may _____ trust in the Lord with all their heart, and lean not on their own understanding. May _____ acknowledge You in all their ways, as You make their paths straight.

Philippians 4:19: *"And my God shall supply all your need according to His riches in glory by Christ Jesus."*

Father I ask You to supply _____'s every need according to Your riches in glory in Christ Jesus.

Romans 8:38-39: *"For I am persuaded that neither death nor life, nor angels nor principalities nor powers, nor things present nor things to come, nor height nor depth, nor any other created thing, shall be able to separate us from the love of God which is in Christ Jesus our Lord."*

Father may _____ remember that You love them no matter what mistakes they have made. For I am sure that neither death nor life, nor angels nor rulers, nor things present nor things to come, nor powers, nor height nor depth, nor anything else in all creation, will be able to separate us from the love of God in Christ Jesus our Lord.

Sometimes You Will Have To Encourage Yourself

The Amalekites had attacked Ziklag, a city in the Negev region, which was southwest of the Kingdom of Judah (1st Samuel 30). They burned it, and took the women and everyone else in it, both young and old, captive. When David and his men got to Ziklag, they found it destroyed by fire and their wives, sons and daughters had been taken captive. David and his men wept until they had no strength left to weep.

Have you ever cried so hard until you had no tears left, no strength left to cry? David had trouble on every side. His family was gone. His men abandoned him and wanted to kill him. Life can deal us a difficult hand. Frustrating situations arise, problems show up that we did not expect. You thought things would be different. You kept believing God through the lies, slandering, accusations. Like Joseph and Abraham, you've been believing God for years to manifest the vision He's given you, and despite your faith and best effort, it just hasn't happened yet.

What do you do when you find yourself in a David situation? What do you do when you've done your best and nothing is going right? What do you do when your finances are out of whack, when your family is messed up, your children are not acting right? What about when the people who should be in your corner turn their back on you? What do you do when people talk about you, mock you, and try to destroy your character? What do you do? You do what David did. David encouraged himself in the Lord.

"And David was greatly distressed... because the soul of all the people was grieved, every man for his sons and for his daughters; **but David encouraged himself in the Lord his God"** – *1 Samuel 30:6*

Think about it. Everything you have been going through should have caused you to fall apart. Yes, you lost some things, but you did not lose your mind or have a nervous breakdown. God can replace and restore what you lost! He can restore your family. David encouraged himself in the Lord. He sought the Lord for instruction. There is a time for crying, but this isn't it. Get up and praise God instead of rehearsing the problem. Crying and complaints don't bring God in. God inhabits the praises of His people. Walk up to the throne of Grace like the child of God that you are and praise God.

> *Praise God instead of rehearsing the problem.*

The battle always begins in your mind and it either increase, or decreases with what you say out of your mouth. Outside of Satan's influences, the next biggest source of most of your problems could be found within you. Proverbs 30:32 warns, *"If you have done foolishly in lifting up yourself, or if you have thought evil, put your hand over your mouth."* Your mouth will follow your mind, so think about good things.

How do you encourage yourself in God? Sometimes it is hard to encourage yourself in the Lord, but you can pull yourself out of despondent situations. Think good thoughts and how God has blessed you. Think about the trials He has brought you through. Remember where He brought you from and think yourself happy! I love music, so I put on some praise music and sing songs of praise that come to my heart. I read and meditate the psalms of praise.

The Bible says in Proverbs 18:21 that life and death are in the power of the tongue. A lot of people mock those of us who believe speaking life into our circumstances will change our circumstance. They label us as name-it-claim-it-blab-it-grab-it folk. Well, call me what you want. I believe what the Bible says. Besides, we know Satan and his demons are behind the mocking, don't we? No matter what you do and how well you do it, there will always be people who will criticize and mock you.

Remember, crying and complaining does not bring God in. God inhabits the praises of His people.

There will always be people who disparage you and attempt to break you down with their words. Try to remember, it is not the person, but demonic forces behind it all (Ephesians 6:12). Speak life, rather than death. Pray that the person Satan is using is released from his bondage and grows stronger in the Lord. Read and meditate on encouraging scriptures. Journal your thoughts and prayers.

Paul wrote the book of Philippians while he was in jail. Rather than focusing on his situation, he focused on God and what God had to say. I spend a lot of time in the Word of God. It's like medicine and food to me. It encourages me. David wrote most of the book of Psalm and encouraged himself. You will find a great deal of encouragement in the Psalms.

Watch who you fellowship with. Attend a Bible believing, Bible teaching church as much as possible. Not only is this sacrifice pleasing unto God, but it's encouraging to be in an atmosphere where His presence is sought. Taking ungodly counsel is one of the worst things a Christian can do when we are struggling.

Ask God to give you friends who can lift you up both physically and spiritually, and encourage you through the times of sorrow. Do things that relax you and bring you joy. I enjoy fishing, sitting on the water, singing karaoke, and writing, of course. What do you like to do to unwind? Take some time to leave the sadness and worry and do what you like to do to unwind.

Scriptures and Prayers

In this chapter are prayers and Scriptures that you can pray, declare, and stand on to help you on this journey. As you pray, declare, and stand, know that I am praying, declaring, and standing with you. Scripture says where two or more are gathered together in His name, He will be in the midst of us. That's the beauty of the power of God, who lives in eternity.

Ephesians 2:6 tells us that God has raised us (Believers) up with Christ and seated us with Him in the heavenly realms. Paul is not speaking literally or physically. He is speaking spiritually. He is saying that by the power of Christ's resurrection we are, through the Holy Spirit, seated spiritually where God and Christ reside, far above all principalities and powers of darkness. Our seated position in Christ is a position of authority, honor, and triumph, not failure, depression, and defeat.

We don't have to try to or pray to be seated there. We don't have to struggle or fight with demons to be seated there. We are already there. This was God's design from the foundation of the world. When we realize our position in Christ, no matter what is going on in our life we will no longer feel defeated.

As you pray these prayers, and declare these Scriptures understand that you are not speaking from your place on earth. You are beside God speaking to Him from your seated position in Christ. The writer of Hebrews 4:14-16 puts it this way: *"Since we have a great high priest who has passed through the heavens, ... let us with confidence draw near to the throne of grace, that we may receive mercy and find grace to help in time of need."* From our seated position in Christ, we only need to turn to God and speak.

As Believers, we are connected in the spiritual realm through Christ. So, you can be in one state, and me in another; you can be reading this book at a certain time, and I have written it, but when you pray this prayer out loud in faith, it is if we are praying the words at the same time together in eternity. So, let us go to the Throne of Grace and seek our Heavenly Father for help in this time of need.

Scriptures To Pray Over Your Children

Hebrews 4:12 says that God's Word is alive and powerful, sharper than a two-edged sword. No word spoken from God will ever be without power. Every word spoken by God will be fulfilled, for God says He watches over His Word to make sure it is fulfilled (Jeremiah 1:12, Luke 1:37). So, you can trust that if God speaks something, it will come to pass. When we believe, speak, and pray the Word of God, we are coming into agreement with God, and His power is released to answer our prayers.

1st John 5:12-14 tells us that we, the children of God, can approach Him with the confidence that whatever we ask according to His will, He hears our prayers, and whatever we ask, we will have. He will answer every prayer in line with His will! It is God's will that every man comes to repentance (2 Peter 3:9).

Here are several Scriptures you can stand on and pray for your children and your family. With each Scripture passage, I include a short prayer example you can pray. Remember, as you stand and pray, I am standing with you. God is listening and setting up situations in their lives so that they can turn to Him. Believe and trust Him.

Proverbs 31:28: *"Her children rise up and call her blessed; Her husband also, and he praises her"*

Heavenly Father thank You that (_____) rises up and call me blessed. In Jesus' name, I pray. Amen.

Psalms 103:17-18: *"But the mercy of the Lord is from everlasting to everlasting on those who fear Him, and His righteousness to children's children, to such as keep His covenant, and to those who remember His commandments to do them."*

Heavenly Father thank You for Your everlasting mercy towards (_____). In Jesus' name, I pray. Amen.

Proverbs 20:7: *"The godly walk with integrity; blessed are their children who follow them."*

Heavenly Father thank that I walk with integrity; and that my children are blessed. In Jesus' name, I pray. Amen.

Isaiah 49:25: *"For thus says the Lord: "Even the captives of the mighty shall be taken, and the prey of the tyrant be rescued, for I will contend with those who contend with you, and I will save your children."*

Heavenly Father thank You for contending with

those who contend with (_____). In Jesus' name, I pray. Amen.

Isaiah 54:13-14: *"All your children shall be taught by the Lord, And great shall be the peace of your children. In righteousness you shall be established; You shall be far from oppression, for you shall not fear; And from terror, for it shall not come near you."*

Heavenly Father thank You that (_____) shall be taught by the Lord, and great shall be (_____)'s peace. In righteousness (_____) shall be established. (_____) shall be far from oppression, and terror. In Jesus' name, I pray. Amen.

Isaiah 65:23-24: *"They shall not labor in vain or bear children for calamity, for they shall be the offspring of the blessed of the Lord, and their descendants with them. Before they call, I will answer; while they are yet speaking, I will hear."*

Heavenly Father thank You that I have not labored in vain or bore children for calamity. My offspring and their descendants are blessed of the Lord. In Jesus' name, I pray. Amen.

Jeremiah 31:16-17: *"Thus says the Lord: "Refrain your voice from weeping, and your eyes from tears; for your work shall be rewarded, says the Lord, and they* *shall come back from the land of the enemy. There is hope in your future, says the Lord, that your children shall come back to their own border."*

Heavenly Father thank You that (_____) shall come back from the land of the enemy. (_____) shall come back to their own border. In Jesus' name, I pray. Amen.

Ezekiel 36:26: *"I will give you a new heart and put a new spirit within you; I will take the heart of stone out of your flesh and give you a heart of flesh."*

Heavenly Father thank You for giving (_____) a new heart and putting a new spirit in (_____). In Jesus' name, I pray. Amen.

Luke 4:18: *"The Spirit of the Lord is upon Me, because He has anointed Me to preach the gospel to the poor; He has sent to heal the broken-hearted, to proclaim liberty to the captives and recovery of sight to the blind, to set at liberty those who are oppressed."*

Heavenly Father thank You healing (_____)'s broken heart and setting (_____) free. In Jesus' name, I pray. Amen.

Acts 2:38-39: *"Then Peter said to them, "Repent, and let every one of you be baptized in the name of*

Jesus Christ for the remission of sins; and you shall receive the gift of the Holy Spirit. For the promise is to you and to your children, and to all who are afar off, as many as the Lord our God will call."

Heavenly Father I thank You that this promise is for me and my children. I ask you to lead (_____) to repentance. May (_____) be baptized in the name of Jesus Christ for the remission of sins; and receive the gift of the Holy Spirit. In Jesus' name, I pray. Amen.

Acts 19:20: *"So the word of the Lord grew mightily and prevailed."*

Father I thank You that Your Word prevails over (_____). In Jesus' name, I pray. Amen.

Scriptures to Declare for Family Healing

In Exodus 15:26 God says tells us *"I am the Lord who heals you."* I am confident that whether it be emotional, physical, mental, or spiritual our Father God can heal us. 1st Peter 2:24 tell us that Jesus bore our sicknesses and carried our pains on the Cross, in order to remove them from us and 'by His stripes we have been healed. Today I pray that the Lord will touch your eyes that you may see Him as He is—your healer. *Then touched he their eyes, saying, According to your faith be it unto you (Matthew 9:29).*

Declare these scriptures over your life and believe for healing for you and your family.

Exodus 23:25 – *"So you shall serve the Lord your God, and He will bless your bread and your water. And I will take sickness away from the midst of you." (NKJV)*

Proverbs 4:20-23 – *"My son, give attention to my words; Incline your ear to my sayings. Do not let them depart from your eyes; Keep them in the midst of your heart; For they are life to those who find them, and health to all their flesh. Keep your heart with all diligence, for out of it spring the issues of life." (NKJV)*

Psalm 30:2 *– "O Lord my God, I cried out to You, and You healed me." (NKJV)*

Psalm 103:2-3 *– "Bless the Lord O my soul and forget not all His benefits; Who forgives all your iniquities, Who heals all your diseases." (NKJV)*

Psalms 107:20-21 *– "He sent His word and healed them, and delivered them from their destructions. Oh, that men would give thanks to the Lord for His goodness, and for His wonderful works to the children of men!" (NKJV)*

Psalms 146:8 *– "The Lord opens the eyes of the blind; the Lord raises those who are bowed down; the Lord loves the righteous." (NKJV)*

Psalm 147:3 *– "He heals the brokenhearted and binds up their wounds." (NKJV)*

2 Kings 20:5 *– "Thus says the Lord, the God of David your father: "I have heard your prayer, I have seen your tears; surely I will heal you. On the third day you shall go up to the house of the Lord."*

Isaiah 38:16 *– "O Lord, by these things men live,*

and in all these is the life of my spirit. Oh restore me to health and make me live!" (ESV)

Isaiah 40:29 *– "He gives power to the weak, and to those who have no might He increases strength." (ESV)*

Isaiah 41:10 *– "Fear not, for I am with you; be not dismayed, for I am your God. I will strengthen you, yes, I will help you, I will uphold you with My righteous right hand." (NKJV)*

Isaiah 53:4-5 *– "Surely He has borne our griefs (sicknesses, weaknesses and distresses) and carried our sorrows and pains (of punishment) ...And with the stripes (that wounded) Him we are healed and made whole. (AMP)*

Isaiah 57:18-19 *– "I have seen their ways, but I will heal them. I will guide them and reward them with comfort. And for those who mourn, I will create reason for praise: utter prosperity to those far and near, and I will heal them, says the Lord."*

Jeremiah 17:14 *– "Heal me, O Lord, and I shall be healed; Save me, and I shall be saved, for You are my praise." (NKJV)*

Jeremiah 30:17 – *"For I will restore health to you, and your wounds I will heal, declares the Lord, because they have called you an outcast: 'It is Zion, for whom no one cares!'" (ESV)*

Matthew 8:17 – *"He Himself took (in order to carry away) our weaknesses and infirmities and bore away our diseases." (AMP)*

Matthew 11:28 – *"Come to Me, all you who labor and are heavy laden, and I will give you rest." (ESV)*

Mark 5:34 – *"And He said to her, "Daughter, your faith has made you well. Go in peace, and be healed of your affliction." (NKJV)*

Luke 6:19 – *"And the whole multitude sought to touch Him, for power went out from Him and healed them all." (NKJV)*

James 5:14-15 – *"Is anyone among you sick? Let*

him call for the elders of the church, and let them pray over him, anointing him with oil in the name of the Lord. And the prayer of faith will save the sick, and the Lord will raise him up. And if he has committed sins, he will be forgiven." (NKJV)

1 Peter 2:24 – *"who Himself bore our sins in His own body on the tree, that we, having died to sins, might live for righteousness—by whose stripes you were healed." (NKJV)*

3 John 1:2 – *"Beloved, I pray that you may prosper in all things and be in health, just as your soul prospers." (NKJV)*

Revelation 21:4 – *"And God will wipe away every tear from their eyes; there shall be no more death, nor sorrow, nor crying. There shall be no more pain, for the former things have passed away." — (NKJV)*

Psalm 91 Prayer Confession

Read Psalm 91.

Heavenly Father, I praise and thank You that I dwell and abide in the secret place of the Most High, under the protection of the Almighty. You are my refuge and shelter from the storm. Thank You for always being with me. You have promised to never leave nor forsake me. Thank You for remaining faithful to Your promise. You are my refuge, my fortress, and my protection from all danger. Surely You shall deliver and rescue me from the snare of the fowler, and from the noisome, deadly pestilence. In You will I trust and put my confidence. Help me to abide and stay close to you.

Father God, I pray for (_____). Cover (_____) with Your feathers, and shield them under Your wings. May Your truth be (_____)' shield and buckler. Deliver me and (_____) from the hand of the enemy. Help us not be afraid or overcome by sickness, disease, and deadly viruses, for you came to give us life and life more abundantly. You are the God who heals all our sickness and disease. By your stripes, we have been healed. I stand on your promises. Help

(_____) to draw closer to You. A thousand shall fall at our side, and ten thousand at our right hand; but let it not come near me or (_____).

May we only see and behold reward of the wicked with our eyes. Give Your angels charge over me (_____), to keep, guard and protect me in all my ways. May they bear us up in their hands, lest we dash our foot against a stone. Because I have set my love upon You Lord, I trust that You will deliver me and (_____), and set us on high, because I have known Your name. With long life You will satisfy me, and (_____), and show us Your Salvation. May we be covered in your precious blood. I pray in the mighty and Name of Jesus Christ. Amen.

Prayer To Restore Broken Family Relationships

Heavenly Father, I bless your Holy name, for you are the only living God. You place us in our families, and You bring families together in unity and love. I thank you for my children and the children of every person praying with me. Thank You for giving us such amazing children. I come together to intercede on behalf of broken family relationships. I pray for myself and every parent and child whose heart is bleeding over their family situation. For that one who is not saved, I ask for salvation for them.

Father, You see the challenges, and You see how the enemy is using guilt, shame, and pride to keep this family apart. Despite what has taken place, I believe through You we can love one another. I ask You to soften the hearts and help everyone concerned to be open to one another so what's been broken can be repaired. Father, please strengthen the bond of this family. Let everything that does not glorify You be uprooted. I speak to anger, jealousy, hatred, hostility, rebellion, vengeance, regret, and unforgiveness assigned to these families and command you to cease your assignment against every member of this family, in Jesus' mighty name. Every wall of division built up between children and their parents be shattered in Jesus' mighty name. Every hindrance working against reconciliation and restoration of this family be removed in Jesus' mighty name. Father, I ask for restoration of all the time that has been lost and stolen. May this family be reconciled in Jesus' name.

Now Father, I praise You that we can see one another through Your eyes and show true mercy, compassion, and love towards one another. I praise You that we are kind and tenderhearted and forgiving towards one another. We declare reconciliation and restoration of this family. Father may Your Name be glorified in this family in the name of Jesus Christ, I pray. Amen.

Struggling With Unforgiveness Prayer

Heavenly Father, Thank you for sending Jesus to the Cross so I can be free from every bondage, including unforgiveness. Forgive me Father for harboring bitterness, and unforgiveness in my heart. I desire to be set free of everything that hinders me, including unforgiveness. Father, You said in Isaiah 43:25-26, "I, even I, am He who blots out your transgressions for My own sake; and I will not remember your sins. Put Me in remembrance; let us contend together; state your case, that you may be acquitted." I come to the Throne of Grace asking for Your help to forgive (_____, _____, _____) who has hurt me.

By faith I receive Your forgiveness, and by faith I extend forgiveness to (_____, _____, _____). Now God, I ask You to heal the wounds caused by the offense and unforgiveness. Create in us a clean heart and renew a right spirit with in us. Thank You that we have everything we need in Christ Jesus to overcome. Empower us by the Holy Spirit to walk free of those behaviors and attitudes that will try to replant themselves in our heart and soul. In the name of Jesus, I bind and cast out bitterness and unforgiveness in Jesus' name. Thank You that bitterness and unforgiveness has been bound in Heaven.

Father, I pray that Your will be done in (_____, _____, _____)'s life in Heaven and on Earth. I pray they turn to You for direction and forgiveness. Help me to see (_____, _____, _____) through Your eyes. I ask for mercy and patience for all concerned while You work Your will in our lives. Show me how to be the loving Christian, You have called me to be in Jesus' wonderful and precious name, I pray. Amen. Hallelujah God! I praise You that I have been set free! I give You all the glory for results that will be clearly seen that all may know that You are God!

If you prayed this prayer from your heart, in faith, I decree and declare that you are delivered from offense, bitterness, and unforgiveness. You are free and ready to forgive offense moving forward quickly.

Prayer For Healing From Rejection

Here is a prayer you can pray for healing from rejection, or pray one of your own:

Heavenly Father, I ask You to forgive me for all my sins. I repent for all sin (name any that the Holy Spirit brings to you). I forgive everyone who ever hurt, rejected or persecuted me, and I ask You, Lord God, to forgive them as well. I bless them all in Jesus' name. I forgive myself, too. Thank You that it is all under the blood of Jesus. Father, those who brought the rejection did not know what the outcome of their actions would do. Show them how the enemy has used them. If they are not saved, I ask for salvation for them. Remove the blinders from their eyes that they might see The Truth.

Father You brought me and my children here for a purpose. Rejection and abandonment are not Your portion for us. I come out of agreement with rejection and abandonment in Jesus' name. I receive only who You say that I am. I pray that Your purpose and Your will for us will be done on earth as it is done in heaven. Thank You for the righteousness and authority that I have in Christ.

Thank You for revealing the rejection that has been holding me and my child(ren) captive. Thank You that Jesus came to set the captive free. He whom the Lord sets free is free indeed. Father, I ask You to reveal to my child(ren) what You have revealed to me about this estrangement. I ask You to uproot anger, bitterness, unforgiveness, and mistrust from us, and release Your unconditional love in us.

In the name of Jesus, I come against rejection, unloved and abandonment, and I bind you from the hearts and minds of me, my child(ren) and grandchild(ren) in Jesus' name. I call unity, unconditional love, adoration, and respect for one another to be bound in our hearts and minds. Help my child(ren) to see that nothing can separate us from You God. It is by Your stripes Lord Jesus that we were healed, and restored. Let wisdom and understanding be released in our life. Let everything that has been lost because of this evil be recovered and restored both in Your sight and in the sight of men. In Jesus' name. Amen!

Prayer to Forgive Someone

Father God, I know You love me, and I love You. Thank you for sending Jesus to the Cross so that I could be free from every bondage including unforgiveness. You said in Isaiah 43:25-26, "I, even I, am He who blots out your transgressions for My own sake; and I will not remember your sins. Put Me in remembrance; let us contend together; state your case, that you may be acquitted."

Father I want to be free from every hurtful or traumatic experience that is holding me in bondage to unforgiveness. I repent of not forgiving, of holding bitterness in my heart, and being upset with people, situations, You and even myself. I ask You to forgive me. Father I realize that the evil done to me was the enemy trying to destroy my offender, and me. I ask for forgiveness for them. I choose to forgive (_____) completely.

I ask You Father to forgive me for releasing any hurt or anger towards them, for any judgmental, and condemning thoughts, words I have spoken to them, and over them. Destroy the destructive seeds, and their harvest that I have planted.

I ask You Father to forgive them, and release them. Let them not be guilty any longer of doing me any harm. I place them in Your Hands Lord Jesus, and I ask You to heal them, deliver them, and set them free, and use them for Your glory.

Father I know You do not make mistakes. You are perfect in all your ways. Forgive me for holding bitterness, and anger in my heart towards You because of situations, and circumstances that did not work out the way I thought they should have. I forgive myself for letting this hurt control me, and for hurting others out of my hurt. I repent of this behavior, and my attitude.

Let the Blood of Jesus Christ purge me from all unforgiveness, bitterness, resentment, and wrath. Help me to know who I am in Christ that I may walk in Your Love. Help me to restore whatever I owe to anyone. Whatever is owed to me by any person in Your strength, and provision may it be released to me, and whatever doesn't come I forgive in the name of Jesus Christ.

Father I receive the finished work Christ has done for healing my emotions, and my physical body. I decree that I am healed in my mind, soul, and body, and command infirmity, and disease to leave from me now in the name of Jesus. I speak restoration, and peace to the areas where the infirmity was.

Thank You Father for giving me beauty for ashes of failure, for replacing mourning, and grief with the oil of joy, and for giving me a garment of praise instead of a spirit of despair. Thank You for forgiving me, and setting me free. I ask You to bind forgiveness in my heart so that when offence comes it will not take root, and I can forgive quickly. In Jesus name I pray, Amen.

Prodigals Coming Home

On January 8th, 2011, I received a word from God through a dream. I dreamed that there was a banquet celebration, and the auditorium was packed with thousands of people. I did not know at the time that it was a celebration for prodigals and their families. There were three men on the platform. Two were sitting and one was standing at the microphone speaking. I instantly noticed one of the young men's shoes and recognized them.

I said, "those are my son's shoes," and I went running through the crowd of people to get to the front to see if it was really him. When I got there, I looked in my son's face. It was really him, and he looked like a totally different person. He was so happy, like joy just surrounded him. The young man at the mic opened up with a prayer and then said, "welcome everyone to the Prodigals Conference Celebration." The people were shouting and celebrating. Flags were flying, horns blowing, and confetti was in the air. It was awesome.

I woke and praised God for the dream and asked what it meant. This is what I heard:

Spread the word ... to those who are waiting on a prodigal to come home, they are on their way. I am ordering their steps right now. They are on their way home.

TESTIMONY: I received this testimony from one of the people I shared the word with. This is what she had to say...

Her testimony.... Praise be to God, for he has answered my prayer. My son re-dedicated his life back to Jesus. Thank you, Angeline, for standing with me in prayer. He told me today that he read your message: Is Hell Real? Is Heaven Real...? Does Life Continue After Death.

He said that article and the prayer, he prayed to God was what led him to give his life to Jesus on today. I wasn't able to be at Church today, but I heard it was an awesome service. While he was at Church, I prayed for him, and asked the Lord to let something be said through the word or something done, that would lead him back into His presence. God has truly answered my prayer. Anyhow, he sends his thanks to you for that message that helped him make the decision. Love, in Christ Jesus! DM

Be encouraged, no matter how far your prodigal child goes, they will find their way back to the path where you both were called to walk. Believe and receive the word that God gave. Praise God for their return! Get their robe and ring ready, they are on coming home! Halleluiah!

Final Thoughts

At the publishing of this book. My sons and I are still estranged. My daughter is still in heaven, and my faith in God is still intact. I still believe and trust that the God who has the power to raise the dead can breathe new life into my family relationship, as well as yours.

I've seen God do too many miracles not to believe that He can heal the family of anyone who believes that He can. Remember, there is a purpose in your pain and healing on the other side. God is not done with you or your estranged child. He hears your heart's cry, and He knows how you long for reconciliation with your child. He answers our prayers in His time, according to His will.

It may take some time before your family comes back together, but continue to believe God is working on your situation and your child. Be patient and let God do what He needs to do with everyone concerned. Do not allow the shocking words of they've said to replay in your mind and dictate your life. Don't stop praying, don't stop praising God for breakthrough. In the meantime, here are some tips to keep in mind.

Don't Feed the Anger

Pain and anger are powerful emotions, and it takes a prayer, persistence, and hard work to repair and rebuild relationships steeped in these emotions. Be willing to fight. This situation can certainly make you angry, but make sure your anger is directed in the right place, at the right one–the devil. Remember we do not wrestle against flesh and blood *[your child]*, but against principalities, against powers, against the rulers of the darkness of this world, against spiritual wickedness in high places. (Ephesians 6:12). Battle in the spirit with the Word of God.

Don't Be Ashamed To Ask For Help

This is a devastating situation to face. If you are not able to handle the situation, don't be ashamed to get help. Connecting with others who understand what you are going through is very helpful. Help can come in many forms depending on your needs. Talking to a Christian counselor, your pastor, or joining a grief therapy or support group can be a great avenue to work through the devastation of being cut off from your child and grandchildren. Don't be embarrassed. Look at it as self-care.

Trust God With Your Child, And Let Him Heal You.

Give your child to God. Take it one day at a time. Try not to worry. Accept and respect their need to walk away. Let go of all unforgiveness and resentment. Focus on your healing. God will take care of all concerned. Pray and confess Psalm 91 over you and them.

Walk In Humility, Own Your Mistakes

Your intent was never to hurt our child(ren), but they may not see things as we do. If they will talk to you, listen, and make an effort to understand what your child has experienced, and own the instances where you may have been in the wrong. Ask God to show you what patterns (strongholds) were at work that led to the separation, and what to do. He will show you. Humble yourself in the ways you approach your relationship. (1 Corinthians 13:4-7)

The Lord bless you and keep you; The Lord make His face shine upon you, and be gracious to you; The Lord lift up His countenance upon you, and give you peace."
– Numbers 6:24-26

About The Author

Angeline L. Williams is a submitted vessel of God who flows in the ministry gifts of prophet, evangelist, pastor, and teacher. Through her insights and revelation, God has led her to influence many individuals into a restored relationship with Jesus Christ. Her passion for God and His Word has led to an anointing to preach and teach the Word of God with authority, revelation, and deliverance. She was licensed and ordained to preach the Gospel in 2002 and walks in the office of prophet, evangelist, pastor, and teacher.

Her messages are illuminated with revelation, personal testimony and a depth of wisdom, and insight resulting from decades of study, and relationship with God. She is available to speak at churches, groups, conferences, workshops, or any place God opens a door. Contact her about speaking at your event at: www.angelinelwilliams.com.

She is the owner of Williams DocuPrep, where

she has been providing self-publishing services to authors, and independent publishers since 2005. Visit her website at www.williamsdocuprep.com to learn more.

Other books by author available online where books are sold.

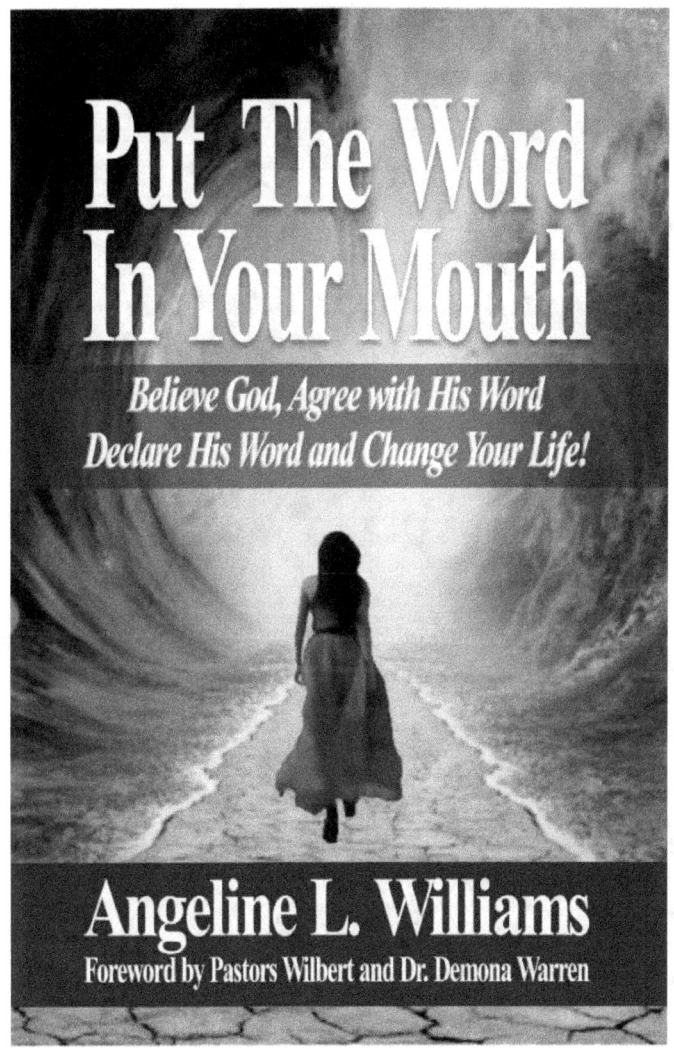

This Means WAR! The Seed Of The Righteous Shall Be Delivered

I Don't Believe In Fairytales

Breaking Anti-Marriage Strongholds

Angeline L. Williams

www.ingramcontent.com/pod-product-compliance
Lightning Source LLC
LaVergne TN
LVHW011832060526
838200LV00053B/3988